An Introduction to Islamic Medicine

An Introduction to Islamic Medicine

by

Hakim Muhammad Salim Khan

Bahr Press 2009

An Introduction To Islamic Medicine
© Salim M Khan 1430 AH/ 2009 CE
First edition published by Routledge, Kegan and Paul 1986
This edition published by Bahr Press in 2009

Published by: Bahr Press
                302 Low Road,
                Norwich, Norfolk,
                NR6 5AW

Website: www.bahrpress.com
E-mail: sales@bahrpress.com

All rights reserved. No part of this publication may be reproduced, stored in any retrieval system or transmitted in any form or by any means, electronic, mechanical, photocopying, recording or otherwise without the prior permission of the publishers.

Written by: Hakim Salim M Khan
General Editor: Abu Bakr Carberry
Typeset by: Abdassamad Clarke

A catalogue record of this book is available from the British Library.

ISBN-13:   978-0-9564513-0-9

Printed and bound by Imprint Digital

Contents

Introduction 1

1. Historical Background 3
Health and medicine in pre-Islamic Arabia 3
Medicine in the early period of Islam 8
The Umayyad period 13
The Abbasid Period 17
Later Works 21

2. Philosophical conceptions of Islamic medicine 25
The problem of knowledge 25
Islam – an integrated unity 27
Tawhid – The first principle and methodology of unification 28
Human Being – a microcosm 31
The *Hakim* – a symbol of unity 32

3. The psychological foundations 35
The human being – an integrated whole 35
The Unity and Diversity of *Nafs* – Self 36
The Origin and Functions of *Ruh* – vital force . 37
Aspects of the Vital Force 38

4. Physiological concepts — 43

- *Arkan* – basic factors — 44
- *Akhlat* – the humours — 46
- *Mizaj* – the temperament — 49
- The temperament of the organs — 51
- The temperament of medicines — 52
- *Aʿdaʾ* – the organs — 53

5. Life Balance — 57

- Ecological considerations — 58
- Mental and emotional factors — 60
- Sleep and wakefulness — 61
- Diet and nutrition — 61
- Physiological movement and rest — 63
- Retention and evacuation — 63

6. Diagnosis — 65

- Indications of health — 65
- Classification of diseases — 66
- Signs of temperaments — 68
- Pulse — 70
- Urine — 72
- Stool — 74

7. Preventative aspects — 77

- Personal Hygiene — 77
- Community health measures — 84
- Fasting – a specific institution of health promotion — 85

8. Principles of treatment — 87

- Management of essential factors — 87
- Treatment through a single remedy — 89

Use of compound medicines	92
The use of the Qur'an in healing	93
Surgical Intervention	95

9. The future of Islamic medicine — 97

Sociocultural implications	97
Economic considerations	99
Implications for peace and happiness	100

GLOSSARY — 101

INDEX — 105

Maps

Map 1 – Pre-Islamic Arabia	4
Map 2 – The Time of the Prophet ﷺ	11
Map 3 – The Umayyad Period	15

Diagrams

Figure 1. The Polarisation of *Quwwah* – Energy	44
Figure 2. The Relative Position of the Elements	46
Figure 3. The Relationship of Seasons, Elements and Fluids	47
Figure 4. Hierarchical Classification of Diseases	67

INTRODUCTION

THE HUMAN BEING – *al-Insān* – has been created in the best possible form and shape. Since he is a vicegerent and custodian – a *khalīfah* in the earth, he needs, as a prerequisite, good health and wellbeing to fulfil his role. Islam provides guidance for all facets of human life and hence lays down general principles in most fields, including health and medicine. There are numerous verses – *āyats* – in the Qur'ān dealing with healing of disease, health, foods and hygiene.

The Prophet Muḥammad ﷺ dealt with many matters specifically dealing with his own, his companions and the general health of the Muslim community. Early in Islamic history, the sayings and actions of the Prophet, peace be upon him, concerning medicine were assembled into authentic collections and remained distinct. This body of knowledge and practice were systematised by Muslim scholars and physicians under a general title known as *aṭ-Ṭibb an-Nabawī*. The medicine of the Prophet ﷺ. Later when Muslims came into contact with other traditions of medicine such as the Greek, Persian, Indian and Chinese traditions, they were synthesised into Traditional Medicine – *Ṭibb*.

This is a brief introduction to the Traditional Medicine of Islam. Which I hope will inspire the reader towards positive health. *An Introduction to Islamic Medicine* will be followed by *The Elemental Dance*. These two works will set the theoretical basis of Islamic Medicine and will be followed by a series of practical books and courses on food, nutrition and exercise insha'Allah.

Salim Khān
13/09/2009
23rd of Ramadhan 1430 A.H

1. Historical Background

"We have sent among you an apostle (Muhammad ﷺ) from among yourselves, rehearsing to you our signs, and instructing you in scripture and wisdom and in new knowledge."

(Sūrat al-Baqarah, *āyat* 150)

Health and medicine in pre-Islamic Arabia

Before considering the genesis and development of Islamic medicine, it would be useful to begin by enquiring into medical conditions before Islam. Pre-Islamic Arabia provides an interesting case study for comparative analysis with later Islamic civilisation. Consideration of the ecological and sociocultural conditions in ancient Arabia would be an appropriate starting point. The Arabian Peninsula, the Arabic term for which is *Jazīrat al-ᶜArab*, is situated on the east of the Red Sea and extends as far as the modern Persian Gulf.[1] The peninsula has considerable variation in climatic and ecological conditions which have influenced both the level and development of medicine.

Within the Arabian peninsula there is to be found one of the great desert regions of the world, covering an area of about 900,000 square miles. It is bordered to the west by the Red Sea, to the north by the Syrian Desert, to the south by the Arabian Sea and the Gulf of Aden

---

1 T.P. Hughes, *Dictionary of Islam*, Cosmos Publications, New Delhi, 1978, p. 17.

An Introduction to Islamic Medicine

Map 1 – Pre-Islamic Arabia

1. Historical Background

and to the east and north-east by the Persian Gulf, the Gulf of Oman and the Arabian Sea. There is almost always a breeze, which changes seasonally to cold or hot gale force winds which chill the body especially at night and roast it during the summer days. The summer heat is intense, with the interior of the peninsula being dry and tolerable. Coastal regions and some highlands, however attain high humidity in summer with dew and fogs at night or in the early morning.

The winters are invigoratingly cool with the coldest weather occurring at Ṭā'if, with several inches of snow and ice. Summer rains in *ar-Rubʿ al-Khālī* accompany the monsoon winds from the Indian Ocean. Dominant winds blow from the Mediterranean, swinging to the east, south-east and south-west in a great arc. Two semi-annual windy seasons occur from December to January and from May to June. These are called *Shamals*, which try the patience of man and beast, are dry and transport huge loads of sand and dust, altering the shapes of sand dunes. Sharp drops in temperature are often followed by rain with wind velocities reaching gale force. On hot days the wind produces myriads of dust devils and the ill-famed mirage.

The vegetation throughout the peninsula is varied. Plants are primarily xerophytic – those which grow in very dry conditions. After the spring rains long-buried seeds germinate and bloom. Date palms are grown in many oases in the desert, and across the peninsula. Also found are rice, alfalfa, barley, wheat, citrus, melons, tomatoes, onions and in the higher regions, peaches, grapes and pomegranates. Fish is in abundance in al-Ḥijāz. Ancient Arabia was well known for its production of myrrh and frankincense, two important ingredients used by the ancient civilisations of Egypt and Greece.[2]

2   N. Groom, *Frankincense and Myrrh*, Longman, London, 1981, p. 96

Arabia has been inhabited by mankind since early times, and consequently has had many influences from different civilisations. Most of the ancient cultures have perished however.[3] The Arabs consider themselves to be descendants of Qaḥṭān and ʿAdnān. From these two ancestors arose numerous tribal units, forever splitting or confederating. Ancient Arabs lived as nomadic and semi-nomadic camel- and sheep-owning pastoralists in villages with agriculture. Their cities have had merchant and religious classes. The Quraysh of Makkah were an important group of tribes who controlled commerce and were in charge of the religious shrine known as the Kaʿbah. They organised two great trading caravans, one setting out in winter for Yemen and the other in summer for Syria. These were huge convoys bringing Oriental and African goods such as perfumes and silk. The visits of these caravans culminated in fairs with pilgrims at Makkah.

Although there have existed monotheistic communities, pre-Islamic Arabia generally was polytheistic. Numerous deities were worshipped, the chief being *al-Lāt, al-ʿUzzā* and *al-Manāt*.[4] Promiscuity was widespread and there were mass exhibitions of nudity and rituals in which both sexes took part.[5] The status and treatment of women was inhuman. Women had no right of inheritance and were considered a commodity. If a man died, the head of the clan would throw his gown over a widow, as a gesture of acquisition which meant that the widow could not remarry anyone except the owner of the gown. If he so wished he could

3   Hughes, op. cit., p. 18
4   Sūrat an-Najm, *āyats* 19-20. Qurʾānic references are quoted in this format, which refers to the Sūrah – chapter, as it is known in Arabic, followed by the number of the *āyat* – sign, which is equivalent to verse or sentence, in this case.
5   A.A. Maududi, *The Philosophy of Hajj*, Idara Tarjuman-ul-Quran, Lahore,1976, p. 20.

1. Historical Background

marry her, or keep her in a state of bondage until she died.[6] Female-child infanticide was common. Newborn girls were buried alive or thrown to their premature deaths from high places.[7] This callous and inhuman practice, left deep emotional trauma on members of the unfortunate families, including the father who had to perform the brutal act.[8] Tribal chauvinism was the hallmark of ancient Arabia. Tribal wars were a common occurrence fermented by interminable vendettas, with the killing of men and enslaving of children and women.[9]

The psychological implications of living in a society of ignorance and injustice were deep insecurity, excessive pride, guilt and dependence on alcohol. Alcohol for the pre-Islamic Arab was a psychological necessity. Life amidst oppression and stress created optimum conditions for the abuse of alcohol. It was so common that the Arabic word *tājir*, which means merchant, became a synonym for the salesmen of *khamr* – alcohol. The shops and bars of these merchants never closed during the day or night and were clearly distinguishable, being designated with special flags.[10] It is within this ecological and socio-economic environment that the level of health and medical knowledge of the pre-Islamic Arabs needs to be located. The general level of health was poor, and harsh climatic conditions were exacerbated by social injustice, poverty and ignorance. Thus it was fertile soil for the growth and proliferation of numerous diseases. The scarcity of a clean and adequate supply of

[6] Sayyid Qutb, *In the Shade of the Qur'ān*, Muslim Welfare House Publishers, London, 1979, p. 66.
[7] M.B. Badri, *Islam and Alcoholism*, American Trust Publications, London, 1978, p. 11.
[8] Ibid. p 11.
[9] Ibid. p 9.
[10] Ibid. p 12.

fresh water was a permanent feature. The nutritional situation was poor, with a shortage of food and a monotonous diet. There were a number of endemic diseases – leprosy, malaria, tuberculosis, rickets, scurvy, numerous eye diseases and gastrointestinal diseases.[11]

The pre-Islamic Arabs were familiar with the workings of major internal organs, although only in general. Surgical knowledge and practices were limited to cauterisation, branding and cupping. The care of the sick was the responsibility of the women. There is no evidence of any oral or written treatise on any aspect of medicine. There was a use of folk medicine, which has interesting connections with magic. It is also interesting to note that pre-Islamic Arabia had contacts with ancient Egypt, Greece, Persia and India, where medicine was highly developed, but there is no material to suggest that it was adopted or utilised by the ancient Arabs. This is particularly surprising in view of the fact that the ancient Arabs were well developed in their poetry.

Medicine in the early period of Islam

The beginning and development of Islamic concepts and practices of health are inextricably interwoven into the general body of Islam. The organic nature of Islam encompasses the core principles of Islamic health traditions. For an understanding of the historical or conceptual aspects of Islamic medicine reference to Islam itself has to be made. The earlier brief sketch of pre-Islamic Arabia, provides a window into the type of society in which the Prophet Muhammad ﷺ lived. The proclamation by Muhammad ﷺ, that he was the final messenger and prophet of Allah to mankind began with the Waḥi – the revelation. Until that day

---

[11] M. Ullman, *Islamic Medicine*, Edinburgh University Press, 1978, p. 1

1. Historical Background

Muhammad ﷺ had lived as a man amongst pagan Arabs, working as a trader. The people of Makkah, where he was born and grew up knew him to be a reflective, kind, and trustworthy man. The forty years that he spent amongst them led them to regard him as *al-Ameen* – The Trustworthy. The foundation of Muhammad's ﷺ message was knowledge based upon higher value. The first revelation placed knowledge as its central focus,

> *"Read! In the name of the Lord who created. Created mankind from a clot of blood. Read! Your Lord is the most bounteous who has taught the use of the pen. Has taught mankind what he did not know."*
>
> (Sūrat al-ʿAlaq, *āyats* – 1-5)

Thus the ignorance-based society of ancient Arabia was faced with Islam, which took revealed knowledge as its basis. The revelation continued to be a regular feature of the next twenty-three years, and the repository of revealed knowledge became the Qurʾān which, as a source of direct and pure knowledge addressed itself to all facets of ancient Arabian belief and conduct. Whilst on one hand the Qurʾān stressed the oneness of Allah and His power, there was also the continued scrutiny of injustices and oppression. The Qurʾān was clear and explicit in referring to these callous practices:

> *"When if one of them receive tidings of the birth of a female his face remains darkened, and he is wrath inwardly. He hides himself from the folk because of the evil of that whereof he has had tidings, (asking himself)! Shall he keep the child in contempt or bury it in the dust. Verily evil is their judgement."*
>
> (Sūrat an-Naḥl, *āyats* – 58-59)

An Introduction to Islamic Medicine

> *"And do not marry those women whom your fathers married ... it was ever lewdness and abomination, an evil way."*
>
> (Sūrat an-Nisā', *āyats* – 4-22)

Muhammad ﷺ continued his work for thirteen years in Makkah and within a decade he was able to attract most of the oppressed people, many of them slaves and poor. The small number of Muslims increasingly became victims of abuse, torture and killing. When the Quraysh saw no success in their nefarious methods they planned to kill Muhammad ﷺ. News of this reached the Prophet ﷺ and he decided to leave Makkah and migrate to the ancient city of Yathrib. (Later Yathrib was referred to as *Madinah al-Munawwarah* – the illuminated city). It is from this event that Islamic dating begins which is known as the *Hijrah*. It was in Madinah that the muslims became a community. As a community they began to develop a tradition of health and well-being that has continued to be practiced in Muslim communities throughout the world. The ecological and climatic conditions of Madinah were much more conducive to life and health than they were in Makkah. Madinah provided the conditions for the unfolding of the Sharīʿah – the Islamic way of life, of which medicine was an integral part. The Qur'ān gave general guidelines and rules on nutrition, cleanliness, marital relations, child rearing, etc. As an example, the Qur'ān established the relationship between nutrition and behaviour. The concepts of *ḥalāl* – lawful and *ṭayyib* – wholesome – were linked to *ʿamal ṣulḥah* – constructive or sound behaviour – and *fisq* – destructive behaviour was related to *ḥarām* – unlawful foods and beverages.

The Messenger ﷺ laid great stress on the importance of sound health amongst his followers. He once said that:

1. Historical Background

Map 2 – Arabia at the Time of Muhammad ﷺ

> "There are two gifts of which many men are cheated, health and leisure."
>
> (*Ṭibb an-Nabī* – as-Suyūṭī[12])

Muhammad ﷺ gave specific instruction on various aspects of health-care and treated people himself. He gave detailed information on specific diseases such as leprosy and infertility, with their causes and treatments. He prohibited certain types of treatments such as cauterisation and magic and introduced more appropriate ones. It was Muhammad ﷺ who told his companions not to embark upon treatment without adequate training. If any patient was harmed then the practitioner would have to pay *diyah* – compensation.[13] The prophet Muhammad ﷺ provided the foundation for a medical tradition that considered a human being in its totality; the spiritual, the psychological and the physical within the context of a social milieu. The environment in Madinah was one where ignorance and oppression was replaced with knowledge and justice. The level of health and well-being of the people of Madinah was such that it appeared miraculous. There was an enormous difference in the level of health between the pre-Islamic era to that in the new community of Muslims. A story from the period illustrates the health conditions:

> "One of the kings of Persia sent to Muhammad ﷺ, a learned physician. He remained in Arabia for one or two years but no one approached him or sought his treatment. At last he presented himself before the Prophet ﷺ, and complained: 'I have been sent to treat your companions but during all this time

---

12 As-Suyūṭī, *Ṭibb an-Nabī*, Osiris, 1962, Vol. 4, p. 51.
13 S.H.H. Nadvi, *Medical Philosophy in Islam and Contribution of Muslim in the Advancement of Medical Sciences*, Academia, University of Durban, Durban, 1983, 7.

no one has asked me to carry out my duties in any respect whatever' to which the Prophet ﷺ, replied: 'It is the custom of these people not to eat until hunger overcomes them and to cease eating while there still remains a desire for food!' The physician answered: 'This is the reason for their perfect health'. He then kissed the ground in reverence and departed."[14]

The period that followed the death of the Prophet ﷺ, is referred to as *al-Khilāfat ar-Rāshidah* – the rightly guided rule. The Prophet ﷺ had created a generation of men and women who became the torchbearers of knowledge and justice in the traditions introduced by him, as he ﷺ put the revelation into practice. It was during this period that the famous medical centre of Jundishapur became part of the Muslim lands and continued to flourish.[15] Companions of the Messenger ﷺ, such as ʿUmar and ʿAlī, may Allah be pleased with them, had become masters of the matter of health and medicine. The prophetic teachings were interpreted by these men. New cities were built according to health principles and Muslim forces and travellers were given specific instructions on the maintenance of good health. The period was an unfolding of the efforts of the Prophet ﷺ, which he had carefully implemented during his entire life. The period of the *al-Khilāfat ar-Rāshidah* was the period of rapid expansion of the Muslim community, with emphasis on collective responses to health and social care.

The Umayyad period

In the forty first year of the Islamic calendar (661

---

[14] C. Elgood, *A Medical History of Persia and the Eastern Caliphate*, Cambridge University Press, 1951, p. 49.
[15] Ibid p. 49.

C.E.) Muʿāwiyah, of the clan Umayyad clan of the Quraysh tribe took over political control. The period that followed is generally referred to as the Umayyad Era. Umayyad rule lasted until 132 A.H. (750 C.E.) in the east and 872 A.H. (1492 C.E.) in the west. It was during the Umayyad period that translations of ancient medical works were begun. The Umayyad prince, Khālid bin Yazīd, grandson of Muawiyah was instrumental in this work. Khālid had a passion for medicine and alchemy. It was he who instructed a group of Greek scholars in Egypt to translate the Greek-Egyptian medical literature into Arabic. These were the first translations made in Islam from one language to another, Khālid himself worked on medicine.[16] It was during this period 120-198 A.H., (737-812 C.E.) that the most celebrated physician and alchemist, Jābir Ibn Ḥayyan lived, a student of the well known Imam, Jaʿfar aṣ-Ṣādiq.

Muʿāwiyah first appointed Ibn Uthal as his personal physician and this became the practice of the Umayyad governors such as Ḥajjāj ibn Yūsuf. However it was Walīd ibn ʿAbd al-Malik who in 88 A.H. (707 C.E.) began a broad health care programme. Walid had homes built for the blind and lepers. He developed specific treatment for the lepers and kept them separate from other patients. He also built a hospital and appointed physicians, who provided healthcare to all citizens and travellers free of charge.[17] This was the beginning of free medical care on a mass level, supported by government funds. Under the Umayyads the Hispanic-Muslim areas of Cordoba and Granada became centres of learning. Economic prosperity, political stability along with an emphasis on knowledge and tolerance

---

16   E.G. Browne, *Arabian Medicine*, Cambridge University Press, 1962, p. 15.

17   M.Z. Siddiqi, *Studies in Arabic and Persian Medical Literature*, Calcutta University, 1959, p. 24.

1. Historical Background

Map 3 – The Umayyad Period

provided ideal conditions for development. The rich and diverse flora of Spain was also a contributing factor. The development of botanical medicine was vast in Muslim Spain. Physicians like Ibn al-Bayṭār, born in Malaga in 598 A.H. (1197 C.E.) spent his early life in Andalusia, identifying and working on different plants. He also wrote a commentary on Dioscorides. His original contribution was the monumental work *al-Jāmiᶜ li Mufradāt al-Adwiyā wa al-Aghdhiyā' – The Complete [book] in Simple Medicaments and Nutritious items*, dealt with some 1400 different items used in treatment. This work became an authoritative contribution to Materia Medica. Other well known physicians were Abū Bakr ibn Samghūn of Cordoba, the philosopher and physician Ibn Bājah and Abū'l-Ḥasan al-Andalūsī who wrote extensively on plant remedies.[18]

Spain had a high level both of general medical practice and surgery. Abū'l-Qāsim az-Zahrāwī, born at Madīnat az-Zahrā', near Cordoba in 325 A.H. (936 C.E.) was one of the most capable surgeons. His systematic work *Kitāb at-Taṣrīf – The Method of Medicine* was the definitive guide for surgeons. The text was accompanied by illustrations of each surgical instrument and was disseminated extensively.[19] In general medicine there were a number of scholar practitioners in Spain writing and practising a wide range of therapies. Abū Marwān ibn Zuhr composed *Kitāb at-Taysīr fi'l-Mudāwāt Wa't-Tadbīr – The Book Facilitating the Study of Therapy and Diet* – and *Kitāb al-Aghdiyah – The Book of Diet*. Ibn Ṭufayl and Ibn Rushd were practising physicians and they also contributed to medical research and literature.

The well known Jewish philosopher and physician

---

18   S.H. Nasr, *Islamic Science*, World of Islam Festival Publishing Co. London 1976, p. 187.
19   Ibid. p. 189.

1. Historical Background

Abū ʿImrān Mūsā ibn Maymūn (Maimonides), who later became personal physician to Salahudin. Maimonides, was an Andalusian and student of Ibn Rushd and Ibn Ṭufayl. He wrote the books *Kitāb al-Fuṣūl* – The Book of Aphorism – and *Kitāb Tadbīr aṣ-Ṣiḥḥah* – The Regime of Health – as well as a number of other specific works. The development of medicine in its varied forms was helped through the particularly important contribution of Umayyad Muslim Spain. There were original contributions to surgery, internal medicine and the creation of new disciplines and specialities such as midwifery.

The Abbasid Period

In 132 A.H. (750 C.E.) the Umayyads, were overthrown by Abū'l-ʿAbbas ʿAbdullah as-Saffāḥ who was descended from al-ʿAbbās ibn ʿAbd al-Muṭṭalib, a paternal uncle of the Prophet Muhammad ﷺ. For the next five centuries it was the Abbasids who dominated the socio-political life of the greater part of the Muslim world. There were major developments during the Abbasid period, particularly in medicine. The transfer of ancient medical knowledge which had begun with the Umayyads acquired new momentum during the Abbasid period. The new impetus came about for a number of reasons. The most significant event was the founding of Baghdad in 186 A.H. (754 C.E.). It was Abū Jaʿfar, known as al-Mansūr, who founded the city of Baghdad on the banks of River Tigris in the most fertile area of Iraq. The site was also chosen for its ideal climate and absence of mosquitos. Al-Mansūr had the city planned in such a manner as to be circular so that all the courtiers might be equidistant from the centre where the palace was built. The city was surrounded by a wall, pierced by four gates named Kufa, Basra,

Khorosan and Damascus for these were the lands and cities to which they led.

The oldest suburb and the first to rise into great importance was that known as Karkh which lay to the south-west of the original walled city and was approached through the Kufa gate. Here was built Bimaristān[20] – the hospital which became the metropolitan hospital and the cradle of the Baghdad school of medicine. Here lectured and practised all the great physicians and surgeons of Baghdad from the time of Bukt Yishu, chief physicians from Jundishapur, to the most celebrated clinician and master of Arabic medicine, Rāzī. The hospital later was referred to as 'The Old Hospital'. The situation of the hospital must have been a delightful one for in front lay the great Karkhaya Canal, a branch of the Isa Canal which joined the waters of the Euphrates to those of the Tigris.[21]

Al-Mansūr, who was the second Abbasid ruler, suffered from dyspepsia throughout his life. Having tried his personal physician, Ibn Allahaj and others in vain, he turned to the physicians of the Jundishapur Medical School. Jundishapur was a flourishing centre of medical learning near the present city of Ahwaz in Iran. It was a cosmopolitan centre attracting scholars and physicians from Egypt, Syria, India, Greece and Persia. The chief physician at Jundishapur was Jurjis Ibn Bukht Yishu whose reputation as a skilled clinician had reached al-Mansūr. Bukht Yishu, stayed in this capacity in Baghdad until near the time of his death; when he asked al-Mansūr's permission to return to Jundishapur in A.H. 149 (C.E. 769).[22]

The second phase in the development of medicine

---

20 A word of Persian origin combining *vimār* – meaning sick and *stan* – meaning place. The word literally means hospital.
21 Elgood, op. cit., p. 70.
22 Ibid. p. 76.

1. Historical Background

dated from the establishment of *Bayt al-Ḥikmah* – the Royal Library – which was based in Baghdad, the Abbasid capital, it became an important centre of translation of medical knowledge. It was within *Bayt al-Ḥikmah* – The House of Wisdom, that systematic and authentic translation as well as compilation was undertaken by competent scholars and physicians. There were separate sections dealing with literature from different languages. Jibrīl Bukht Yishu, a descendant of Bukht Yishu migrated to Baghdad from Jundishapur. He established a medical practice in Baghdad, and began writing and teaching. Yuhanna ibn Masawayh, whose father worked at Jundishapur also gained fame in Baghdad as an ophthalmologist. Ibn Masawayh became responsible for the translation of Greek texts and manuscripts into Arabic. Ḥunayn ibn Isḥāq, a student of Ibn Masawayh was a prolific writer on medicine. He translated the work of Hippocrates, Galen and the Alexandrian summaries from Greek into Arabic. His original contribution was *Kitāb al-ʿAshr Maqālāt fi'l ʿAyn* – *Ten Dissertations on the Eye*. Thābit ibn Qurrah compiled a work titled *The Treasury*, which became the standard text on medicine. ʿAlī ibn Rabban aṭ-Ṭabarī wrote the well known *Firdaws al-Ḥikmah* – *The Paradise of Wisdom*. Aṭ-Ṭabarī used the medical contribution directly from Indian works. There were attractions in Abbasid Baghdad for physicians and scholars, many of them had been invited to work for their patrons. An Indian physician Mankha, was active in Baghdad translating Indian medical classics into Arabic.[23]

Within the two centuries under the Abbasids, the medical heritage of ancient civilisations became accessible to Arabic scholars. In the *Bayt al-Ḥikmah* – "The House of Wisdom", scholars could work with all

---

23 Ibid., p, 175.

the necessary provisions and substantial income. The task of stocking the academy with new manuscripts became considerably facilitated due to the recent discovery of paper manufacture. Although paper was a Chinese discovery, it was introduced to the Muslim world when Samarqand was captured and the first paper manufacturing factory was established in Baghdad in 174 A.H. (794 C.E.).

The two centuries of Abbasid rule had made accessible to the Arab-speaking physicians the greater part of the classical medical heritage. The link in this important process was the new-found city of Baghdad. The next three centuries saw the synthesis and creation of new therapies. There were a number of original thinkers and practitioners whose contribution to Islamic medicine remains alive and pulsating. Muḥammad ibn Zakariyyā ar-Rāzī was born in Rai in Persia. He studied music, alchemy and later medicine. He became responsible for the main hospital in Baghdad. He was a prolific medical scholar leaving many classical works such as the encyclopaedic *al-Ḥāwī – Contents on Internal Medicine*. One of the most illustrious figures of this period was Abū ʿAlī ibn Sīnā, known as 'the Prince of the Physicians'. Ibn Sīnā was born in 370 A.H. (980 C.E.) near Bukhara and travelled through Persia until his death in 428 A.H. (1037 C.E.).[24] Ibn Sīnā's most celebrated work is *al-Qānūn fi'ṭ-Ṭibb – The Canon of Medicine*. Baghdad continued to be a centre of learning with a high level of medical practice and teaching. It was during the Abbasid period that the examination and licensing of physicians and surgeons was formally organised. However the central role of Baghdad became less important after it was devastated by Hulagu, grandson of Ghengis Khān in 640 A.H. (1240 C.E.).

24 M.H. Shah, *The General Principles of Avicenna's Canon of Medicine*, Naveed Clinic, Karachi, 1966, p 439.

1. Historical Background

LATER WORKS

After the devastation of Baghdad the history of Islamic medicine becomes more diverse. Fortunately, before the invasion of Baghdad there had already been founded centres of medical learning in other parts of the Muslim world. The core concepts and practices of Islamic medicine continued to be common to various areas, although there were unique characteristics to each locality. Iran continued to be a source of medical inspiration for many years with notable physicians such as Sayyid Zayn ad-Dīn Ismāʿīl al-Ḥusaynī al-Jurjānī who wrote *Dhakhīrah Y Khwarzam – The Treasury of Medicine*, dedicated to the King of Khwarzam. In Samarqand, Abū Ḥāmid Muḥammad as-Samarqandī composed *Kitāb al-Asbāb wa'l-ʿAlāmāt – The Book of Causes and Symptoms*. The Saffavid period continued with many new works on gynaecology. In Iran, it was from the reign of Nadir Shah onward that European medicine was introduced through the newly founded Centre, Dār al-Funūn in Tehran.[25]

In Egypt, under the Fatimids, Cairo became a centre of learning and started to attract competent physicians such as Maimonides who came over from Cordoba, Spain. Other reputable practitioners were al-Laṭīf al-Baghdādī, ʿAbd ar-Raḥīm ad-Dakhwar and the famous medical historian, Ibn Abi ʿUsaybiah. The physician-surgeon ʿAlā' ad-Dīn ibn Nafīs was the first to explain accurately the minor circulation of the blood. He was born in Damascus in 607 A.H. (1210 C.E.) and died in 687 A.H. (1288 C.E.).[26]

Ottoman Turkey was also an important centre of Islamic medical knowledge. The Turks built numerous hospitals which were open to all people, following the

25 Nasr op. cit., p 187.
26 S.H. Nasr, *Science and Civilisation in Islam*, Harvard University Press, 1968, p. 213

general practice in other parts of the Muslim world. The hospitals were generally regulated by trust deeds as welfare institutions. There were hospitals and medical schools built by the sultans which were both civic and military. A number of the later hospitals are still in active use in Turkey today. The language of medical instruction in Turkey was originally Arabic and was later changed to Turkish. Many of the well known physician wrote both in Arabic and Turkish. Initially, Turkish physicians travelled to Egypt but later Turkey became a centre for higher medical knowledge. The well known Turkish practitioners were many including Ḥakīm Hae Pasha and Ayindoglu Umar Bey, known as the Ibn Sīnā of Anatolia. It was a Turkish physician who first used smallpox vaccinations in 1059 A.H. (1679 C.E.). During Sultan Maḥmūd II's reign 1209 A.H. (1829 C.E.) European medicine came to be taught by Dr. Bernard from Vienna, in French.[27]

The history of Islamic medicine in the Indo-Pakistan subcontinent is closely related to that of Iran. The primary language of Mogul India was Persian. Initially the language of medicine was Persian, although later Indian scholars translated medical literature into Urdu and also developed new methods. Indian physicians began to work closely with the Ayurvedic physicians which gave new impetus to Islamic medicine. India became the centre of medical learning with both traditions working very closely and at times in the same institutions and associations. India and Pakistan produced some of the most eminent physicians in later times. Akbar Arazani, author of *aṭ-Ṭibb al-Akbar* – 'The Great Medical Work' – was one of the last physicians of the Mogul period. Ḥāfiẓ Muḥammad Ajmal Khān of Delhi, known as *Masīḥ al-Mulk* – Healer of the Nation, one of his outstanding students and *ḥakīm*, Ḥakīm

[27] M. Said, Hamdard Medical Digest, 1959, Vol 1-2, p. 136.

1. Historical Background

Muḥammad Hussain known as *Shifā' al-Mulk* – Healer of the People, were the most celebrated custodians of traditional Islamic medicine in the twentieth century.[28]

---

[28] Personal communication and discussion with Ḥakīm Muḥammad Nabi Khān and Ḥakīm Muḥammad Riaz Qersih Ṣāḥib, may Allah have mercy upon them.

2. Philosophical conceptions of Islamic medicine

"... This day I have perfected your way of life for you, completed my favour upon you and have chosen for you Islam as your way of life ... "

(Sūrat al-Mā'idah, *āyat* – 3)

The problem of knowledge

The *Mathnāwī* of Jalāluddīn Rūmī, a classic of wisdom, contains a story called 'The disagreement as to the description and shape of the elephant'. It runs as follows:

"The elephant was in a dark house. Some people had brought it for exhibition. In order to see it, many people were going, every one, into that darkness and, as seeing it with the eye was impossible, each one was feeling it in the dark with the palm of his hand. The hand of one fell on the trunk. He said, 'This creature is like a water pipe.' The hand of another touched his ear: to him it appeared to be like a fan. Another handled its leg and said, 'I found the elephant shape to be like a pillar.' Another laid his hand on the back – he said, 'Truly this elephant is like a throne.' Similarly, when anyone heard a description of the elephant, he understood it only in respect of the part that he

25

had touched. On account of the diverse points of view, their statements differed. One man entitled it *Dāl*, another *Alif*. If there had been a candle in each one's hand, the difference would have gone out of their words. The eye of sense perception is only like the palm of the hand: the palm hath not power to reach the whole of the elephant."

The genius of Rūmī has penetrated to the centre of the problem of knowledge. Each hand fumbles over some part of the elephant, each proclaiming what they have discovered, and none is able to relate the part to the whole. The invention of instruments that render the senses a thousand or more times acute does not reduce the difficulties: if anything it increases them. Because of minute examination one is unable to listen to what is being said at the other end of the elephant. Even if it is possible to spare the time to study different disciplines or specialities, the search for knowledge has become so intense, so much data and observations have been accumulated, that no person can ever hope to know all that others have recorded. The prospect of synthesising so much data seems an impossible task. It would seem that the very existence of an elephant has been forgotten. Consequently efforts are solely upon compilation of vast catalogues of observation on the trunk, legs or tail as the case may be.

This is the unsatisfactory state in which the whole body of knowledge finds itself. It is equally true of medical science: medicine studies the human being, which is an indivisible whole of such enormous complexity that it is impossible to grasp the truth about him. Modern science, therefore, has taken him to pieces in order to study each piece separately. The modern physician, called upon to deal with a sick human being, is confronted with a truly formidable task. What renders this task so difficult is the fact that

2. Philosophical conceptions of Islamic medicine

the physician is unaware of what a normal human being is, still less a sick one. He has an acquaintance with the organs of a human being and has an idea of how they work, but of the reality or nature of the human being himself, he is woefully and confessedly ignorant. Since the Renaissance in European society the fundamental conceptions of creation, life and human being have developed in mechanistic and materialistic paths to the exclusion of any higher values. In general, this view of the world has created fundamental problems, both technological and psychological, which have placed mankind on the edge of an abyss. In this context, the ethical and holistic perspective of the Islamic tradition of health provides hopeful insights.

Islam – an integrated unity

Any comprehensive tradition of medicine has a network of independent concepts and practices through which the origin, understanding, treatment and prevention of illness and maintenance of health is explained. In reality there are close and intimately inseparable relations between the conception of a human being and health and disease.

Islam, as *Dīn al-Fiṭrah* – the natural way of life, has its own paradigms of knowledge. The Islamic view of reality, provides a matrix in which central problems of knowledge are illuminated. Islam as a complete way of life has its own understanding of various aspects of life, including the maintenance of health and the alleviation of disease. For an understanding of the Islamic philosophy of medicine it is necessary to have familiarity with the core values of Islam regarding the nature of creation, the position of humankind and the path of well-being.[29] Thus the health of an individual or

---

29 The essential philosophical concepts are derived from the

a society can only be located within a context of Nature, society and man, as medicine is a facet of an integral view of reality. The essential outline of philosophical tradition of Islamic healing is illuminated by the light of *waḥy* – revelation. The cosmos is the context and the human being is the subject. This philosophical perspective considers that genuine health and happiness is the natural state of existence. However, it can only be maintained or acquired by observing the fundamental laws of creation. It is in this respect that medicine needs to be located.

TAWHID – THE FIRST PRINCIPLE AND METHODOLOGY OF UNIFICATION

Islam as a universal principle lies in the nature of creation and comprehends a human being in its totality. The whole edifice of Islam is based on an understanding of *tawḥīd* – a primordial concept of the oneness and unity of all creation. The created universe is perceived through this principle. Unity is a world view and a mode of comprehension, a substratum upon which Islamic sciences in general, and medicine in particular, rests. Unity as a method perceives the cosmos as a dynamic, integrated and purposeful whole. It is a method of integration and means of becoming whole and realising the profound oneness of all creation. Every aspect of Islamic thought and action rotates around the doctrine of unity, which Islam seeks to realise in a human being in his inward and outward life. Every manifestation of human existence is organically related to the *shahādah* – witnessing – there is no deity except Allah, which is the most universal way of expressing unity. From

---

Qur'ān, the Ḥadīth – 'Traditions and Sayings of the Prophet, ﷺ', and the works of Islamic scholars such as al-Ghazālī and Ibn ʿArabī.

2. Philosophical conceptions of Islamic medicine

this perspective the universe is viewed as a unity with varying levels of intelligence and will, in varying degrees. The universe is all the beings who populate the immensity of the skies, who constitute the regions of multiplicity which extend to the spheres, the stars, the elements, their products and humankind.

From this cosmological view the creation is divided into relative and continuing aspects, influencing each other: *ghā'ib* – unseen or hidden – and *ẓāhir* – manifest. The manifest aspect of existence is accessible to sense perception and experience. These outer manifestations are *āyats* – signs of the true essence. The outer and sensory manifestations are traces of primary and unseen reality. In this paradigm of knowledge there is an internal unity and integration between various levels of existence. Consequently, this philosophical and conceptual approach towards an understanding of reality has its own unique methodologies. One of the methods extensively employed by the scholars and practitioners is the symbolic language of analogy. The classical analogy of macrocosm and microcosm suitably illustrates the point.

In medical practice the analogy of the human being with the cosmos is used extensively:

> "The body itself is like the earth, the bones like mountains, the brain like mines, the belly like the sea, the intestines like the rivers, the nerves like the brooks, the flesh like dust and mud, the hair on the body like plants, the places where hair grows like fertile land and where there is no growth like saline soil. From its face to the feet the body is like a populated state, its back like a desolate region, its front like the east, back the west, right the south, and left the north. Its breath is like the wind, words like thunder, sounds like thunderbolts. Its laughter

like the light of noon, its tears like rain, its sadness like the darkness of night and its sleep like death. As its awakening is like life, the days of its childhood are like spring, youth like summer, maturity like autumn and old age like winter. Its motions and acts are like the motions of stars and their rotation. Its birth and presence are like the rising of stars and its death and absence like their meeting.[30]

The analogy is of profound significance, with practical implications in diagnosis and treatment. The micro-macro idea allows, through its profundity, the practitioner to penetrate beyond the physical realm. In the study of both nature and man, this idea provides the link in showing the unicity of creation, whilst demonstrating and enabling the inward relationship between them. Traditionally, the universe is macrocosm, or *al-Insān al-Kabīr* – 'the great man'. The universe is seen as one integrated body in all its spheres and gradation. It is also considered that the world has one *nafs* – life force, whose powers run into all the organs and cells of its body, similar to the human being. In this respect analogies from the microcosms can illustrate another difficult concept. As an example, the relationship of the universal life force of the universe, described above, becomes vivid and easy to comprehend when compared to the human life force and the human body. Conversely analogies from the universe can be used to explain the human being by correspondence drawn from the outer aspect. This is the broad context within which each individual is located. The multifarious influences from the different levels of the cosmos are an important consideration in the ability of man towards the maintenance of an equilibrium.

---

[30] S.H. Nasr, *An Introduction to Islamic Cosmological Doctrines,* Thames and Hudson, London, 1978. p. 101 ... 102.

2. Philosophical conceptions of Islamic medicine

HUMAN BEING – A MICROCOSM

The creation of a human being occupies an important place in the philosophy of Islamic medicine. The origin, nature and purpose of humankind are important guidelines for the practitioner in enabling the patient towards health and well-being. The story of human creation is vividly illustrated:

> "Man did We create from a quintessence (of earth); then We placed as (a drop of) sperm in a place of rest, firmly fixed; then We made the sperm into a clot of congealed blood; then of that clot made a (foetus) lump; then made out of that lump bones and clothed the bones with flesh; then We developed out of it another creature. So blessed be Allah, the Best of creators."
>
> (Sūrat al-Mūminūn, *āyats* – 12-14)

Like all of creation, human beings are created to live and function harmoniously within themselves and their surrounding. Each person individually, and mankind collectively, are endowed with an awareness and a consciousness. Creation is an *amānah* – trust – placed with mankind ideally and according to a design, mankind has the potential to uplift and develop himself and the rest of creation, or degrade and abase himself and his environment. Thus, each person individually and human beings collectively, are simultaneously affecting and are affected by their environment. The purpose of human beings is ʿ*ibādah* – serving and harmonising with the divine will. The outcome and result of ʿ*ibādah* is an unconditional state of *sakīnah* – peace and tranquillity. The concept of ʿ*ibādah* is a fundamental tenet of Islamic medical philosophy. Any evaluation of health has to take into account this central concept, as it is the key to an entire human integrity or dissipation at all levels of the being, be they psycho-physiological or psycho-spiritual. It is in this broad holistic perspective that the tradition of Islamic medicine is defined and located.

Aṭ-Ṭibb al-Islāmī – Islamic medicine, is the body of practices that deal with the different states of *insān* – the human being in health and disease. Its purpose is to maintain health and endeavour to restore it whenever lost. Health is a dynamic state in which all functions are carried out in a *ṣaḥīḥah* – correct or sound – and *salīmah* – whole – manner.[31] This can be elaborated in that health is a dynamic condition of *iʿtidāl* – balance. It is a harmonious state of forces and elements composing the human being, as well as being external to him in conformity with the constructive principle in nature; each individual as a purposeful and integrated unity is always acting with innate intelligence to maintain a complete and dynamic condition of balance at different levels.

The Hakim – a symbol of unity

The holistic perspective and unity is reflected in the discipline of Islamic medicine. Indeed the principle of unity permeates and goes deep into the very structure of the cosmos and the human self. The practitioner of this medicine is a classical example. In this figure of the *ḥakīm* – sage and physician – one can see the unity of the sciences, as so many branches of a tree whose trunk is the wisdom embodied in the *ḥakīm*. The *ḥakīm* has always established the unity of the sciences in the minds of students by the very fact of his teaching all of the sciences as many different applications of the same fundamental principles. The Islamic teaching system as a whole and classification of the sciences which

---

31 Ibn Sīnā, *The General Principles of Medicine*, Naveed Clinic, Karachi, 1966, p 142.

2. Philosophical conceptions of Islamic medicine

forms the matrix are themselves dependent upon this figure of the *ḥakīm*.[32]

---

[32] S.H. Nasr, *Science and Civilisation in Islam*, Harvard University Press, 1968, p. 184.

3. THE PSYCHOLOGICAL FOUNDATIONS

"The question of the unity of the Divine Principle and the consequent unicity of nature is particularly important in Islam where the idea of unity (*at-tawḥid*) overshadows all others and remains at every level of Islamic civilisation the most basic principle upon which all else depends."

Sayyed Hossein Nasr

THE HUMAN BEING – AN INTEGRATED WHOLE

The paradigm of Islamic psychology is essentially derived from the core of Islamic traditions especially in the analysis of *nafs* – the self – and the means by which it can acquire its purpose, a state of unconditional tranquillity. *Qalb* – the heart, a non-material principle, is the essence of self and has predominant control of the life of an individual, by which reality is perceived and interpreted. The heart, from a traditional Islamic perspective, represents the whole human being in relation to *ad-dunyā* – the immediate condition and *al-ākhirah* – the approaching reality.[33] It is this essence which distinguishes human beings from all other created beings and constitutes the excellency which enables him to realise the truth. The heart is the point of union between *jism* – the

---

[33] Al-Ghazālī, *Kimya-I-Sadat*, Sheikh Ghulam Ali and sons publishers, Lahore, 1977, p. 60.

body, and *rūḥ* – the spirit. In the Islamic order of creation the heart is the non-material centre of the human organism, that which registers and reflects conditions of consciousness. Changes can be initiated by external or an internal stimulus. It is on this plan that the essential functions such as the will, thinking and synthesis take place. Disturbance of these core functions constitutes a fundamental imbalance and disharmony within an individual. The heart is the centre of an organic whole of the psyche and the soma that guides, directs and controls the human organism towards the realisation of, and unification with, the truth.

The Unity and Diversity of Nafs – Self

The most tranquil and balanced state of the self is *an-nafs al-mutma'innah*.[34] This is the ideal to which the self can aspire and as a consequence of this state there is complete harmony within an individual in all realms of his functioning. The next state is one which is out of balance but has the ability and desire to be in tune; this condition is referred to as *an-nafs al-lawwāmah*, the reproachful condition in which the self is active in gaining its lost balance.[35] The most unhealthy condition of the self is *an-nafs al-ammārah*.[36] This is the condition of insensitivity and complete imbalance towards the destructive side of the spectrum. Thus we can see how the notion of tranquillity and balance is a central component in evaluation of the human condition and how it has far reaching consequence regarding the health of an individual.

---

[34] Sūrat al-Fajr, *āyat* – 27.
[35] Sūrat al-Qiyāmah, *āyat* – 2.
[36] Sūrah Yūsuf, *āyat* – 53.

3. The psychological foundations

THE ORIGIN AND FUNCTIONS OF RUH

Muslim physicians consider man as a psychosomatic unity endowed with a self-directing, purposeful *rūḥ*, or vital force which issues from the left ventricle of the heart and enables activity, growth, forms and functions appropriate to the purpose of creation.[37] The vital force has a manifestation of a combination of *laṭīf* – subtle particles of the *akhlāṭ* – the primary fluids and consequently the quantity and quality can be modified with appropriate changes in nutrition, medication and psycho-emotional factors. The vital force diffuses itself into the remotest parts of the organism and resembles the sun in luminosity. The vital force functions as an integrated totality in a systematic manner, according to the laws of creation. An imbalance or disharmony within the vital force is the very beginning of disease, prior to any manifestation of pathology. Thus disease per se begins with the vital force, whilst functional or structural changes are secondary. The nature of the vital force is dynamic, penetrating and animating every organ and particle of human being. The existence of vital force as an integral guiding principle within the human organism provides the Islamic science of healing with a logical, appealing and therapeutically useful entity whilst providing a conceptual basis for the unity of disease. We can examine, in some detail the various physiochemical functions of the vital force as it moves into different parts of the human organism. Although the vital force is one pulsating entity, in actual practice it has been divided into different parts on account of its functions, thus making it much more valuable in diagnosis and therapy.

---

[37] Ibn Sīnā, *Kitāb al-Adwiyā al-Qalbiyah*, Iran Society, Calcutta, 1956, p. 1.

ASPECTS OF THE VITAL FORCE

That part of the vital force which issues forth from the left side of the heart is referred to as *rūḥ ḥaywāniyyah* – the vital faculty, due to its role as a vehicle for the maintenance of life within the human being. One of the major functions of the vital faculty is that it enables organs to receive life. The expansion and contraction of the vital force are subsumed by this faculty too.

Rūḥ ṭabayyah – the natural faculty, is of two types; that which is responsible for the preservation of the individual, centred in the liver, and that which is responsible for the preservation of the species, located in the testicles, or ovaries in the case of the female. The first type is essentially concerned with nutrition and growth while the second type is concerned with reproduction. For nutrition and growth to take place there are a number of processes that are necessary. Attraction, a process by which food is brought into the cells and tissues and is retained by retentive force until it has been digested by a digestive faculty. When the food is suitably digested it is assimilated and integrated into various cells and tissues.

Here *al-quwwah al-mughayarah* – the individuation faculty operates throughout the human body, functioning differently in the various organs according to their unique requirements. This need can be functional or structural. Each organ or system of the organism has an inherent natural faculty which enables it to make suitable changes in the nutrient. The process renders them one with each other in such aspects as colour and consistency. Conditions such as leucoderma, as an example, where absorption and assimilation are normal but wholeness is lacking, indicates defective individuation. Finally, the expulsive faculty is a process whereby non-nutritive matter,

3. The psychological foundations

nutritive material in excess and material that has served its useful purpose and is no longer required is eliminated. It is useful to remember that waste matter is generally expelled through natural channels of elimination. However, when such outlets are not functioning properly, waste matter is diverted to an inferior organ, rather than a superior one, to a soft rather than a hard organ and to a less important organ than a more important one. This whole strategy of the vital force indicates inherent wisdom to safeguard the core of the person from disease.

For the successful perpetuation of the species there needs to be generative and formative faculties. The generative faculty is referred to as the faculty of primary individuation and is inherent within the semen. It is the first to appear in the development of the embryo. The generative faculty deals with the formation of male and female germinal fluids which have the ability to develop the various specialised cells, tissues and organs. The formative faculty gives shape, appearance and texture to the various parts, in conformity with the laws of creation.

That aspect of the vital force which is responsible for movement and sensation, and consists of cognition and conation is *rūḥ nafsāniyyah* – the nervous faculty, and is centred in the brain. Cognition is divided into two aspects: *Ẓāhir* – the external or conscious, and *ghā'ib* – the internal or unconscious. External cognition operates by means five sense, namely vision, hearing, smell, taste and touch. Some consider touch to be a sense that has pain, temperature, smoothness or roughness, softness or hardness as its sub-divisions, thus considering eight senses in total. Conation is the process by which joints and organs are moved. This results from the transmission of impulses to muscles by means of corresponding nerves. Each muscle has its own mode of movement and activity, which is initiated by thinking, which is in turn subordinate to will.

Internal cognition or perception is a complex and intricate affair which has a number of processes. The composite sense is one that is located within the interior ventricle of the brain, and receives any image apprehended by the external senses and combines them into a coherent mental picture. The images formed are stored after their disappearance from the consciousness and this is carried out by *quwwah mutafakkirah* – thinking, which is different from imagination. When it serves *al-quwwah an-nāṭiqiyah* – the rational mind, then it is termed thinking whereas when it serves *wahm* – intuition, then it is referred to as imagination. There is a difference between thinking and imagination in that thinking can re-arrange the impressions and can produce not only images derived from perception but can occasionally add something more which is contrary to all perception, e.g. seeing an emerald mountain. Thinking is centred within the mid-ventricle of the brain.

Intuition is the process which gives an impetus to that which had no perceptual basis and is impelling and directive in many ways. Intuition can be a source of information protecting that which it believes to be important. Intuition's function is to discover the suprasensual ideas and it is located within the extremity of the middle ventricle of the brain. Memory is located within the posterior ventricle of the brain, together with recall. Reasoning is a component of internal cognition. These various processes originating from the external and internal sources are referred to the heart which in the light of *ʿaql* – an apprehending light, deals with them according to the condition of the self.

3. The psychological foundations

Thus we begin to see that the idea of unity permeates throughout Islamic psychology with the heart as its pivotal point.

4. Physiological concepts

> *"And they shall be made to drink a cup the mizāj (temperament) of which shall be Ginger"*
>
> (Sūrat al-Insān, *āyat* – 17)

The fundamental concepts in Islamic Medicine have their basis within a traditional Islamic cosmology, a matrix for all the Islamic sciences. The manifestation of existence by being is a result of the polarisation of material prima into *quwwah* – energy.[38] Muslim physicians and scientists subscribe to theory that the highest level of organisation of the cosmos is not physical but one concerned with complex energy structures. The conception of the universe in terms of energy also extends to other organisms including human beings. This approach was developed by creating a spectrum for measuring the quality of energy. The four primary qualities of heat, cold, moisture and dryness are used as a qualitative aspect of measurement, heat and cold being active and moisture and dryness passive. The concept of energy and its qualitative aspect were further developed into four basic universal symbols of the primary elements. The macrocosm, of which the human being constitutes the microcosm, is considered the resultant of the interplay between these four primeval elements which are united in an unvarying pattern.

---

[38] Energy is a central concept in Islamic medicine.

```
              Primal Hot
                  |
                  |
Primal Dry————————+————————Primal Moist
                  |
                  |
              Primal Cold
```

Figure 1. The Polarisation of *Quwwah* – Energy

Arkan – basic factors

The *arkān* – the elements; this is a symbolic reference to actual fire, air, water and earth and not identical per se.[39] The elements are simple bodies, primary components of all minerals, plants, animals and human beings. The various orders of being depend for their existence on a particular combination of the elements. The elements are subservient to the action of nature, a force present in all beings which directs and guides them.

"The earth is the warp and weft of the body.

Heaven is man, and earth woman in character;

whatever heavens sends it, earth cherishes,

when earth lacks heat, heaven sends heat,

when it lacks moisture and dew, heaven sends them."[40]

---

[39] O.C. Gruner, *The Cannon of Medicine of Avicenna*, Augustus M. Kelley, New York 1970. p. 34.

[40] Ibid. p. 35.

4. Physiological concepts

Earth is an element normally situated at the centre of all existence. In its nature it is at rest and all other elements naturally tend towards it, however great a distance away they might be. This is because of its intrinsic weight. Earth is cold and dry. In the scheme of creation it serves the purpose of rendering things firm, stable, lasting and heavy. It is by means of the earthly element that other parts are fixed and held together in a compacted form. Thus it is due to earth that the outward form is maintained. The vibration rate of the earth is slow. It is passive and receptive in nature like the female principle in creation.

Water is a simple substance whose position in nature is exterior to the orbit of earth and interior to that of air. This is due to its relative density. It is cold and moist. The purpose of water in the scheme of creation lies in the fact that it lends itself to dispersion. Water provides, in the construction of things, the possibility of being moulded and shaped without permanence. Water being moist allows shapes to be readily fashioned. Water is the source of life as well as being essential to life.

Air is a simple substance, occupying the position above the sphere of water and beneath that of fire. This is due to its relative lightness. Air is hot and moist. In nature, in the process of creation of things is to rarefy and render things finer, lighter and more delicate.

Fire is a simple substance, occupying a position in nature higher than that of the other three elements. Fire is hot and dry. The part fire plays in the creation of things is that it matures, refines and intermingles with all things. Its penetrative power enables it to permeate the substance of air. It thus subdues the coldness of earth and water and enables their integration into various compounds. Earth and water are required for the formation and the stability of the organs whereas the lighter elements, air and fire, are necessary for

Figure 2. The Relative Position of the Elements

the production and the movement of the vital forces aiding the activity of the organs.

AKHLAT – THE HUMOURS

Akhlāṭ are the biological application and extension of the elements. Muslim physicians conceived of the human body as a combination of *al-akhlāṭ al-arbaʿah*, the four primary fluids, normal and abnormal. Normal fluids are capable of being assimilated and integrated into tissue or energy, whilst abnormal fluids are unsuitable for assimilation and can be a source of imbalance and ill-health. There are four primary fluids: *Sawdah* – Black Bile, *Bulghum* – Phlegm, *Dam* – Blood and *Ṣafrah* – Yellow Bile. These four primary fluids in their normal state are responsible for the physiological, morphological and energy requirements of the body. Since the mucus membrane of the mouth is in direct continuity with the mucosa of the stomach,

4. Physiological concepts

```
              Bile
               △
              Fire
               |
            Summer
Blood ←── Air ── Spring ┼ Autumn ── Earth ──→ Black bile
            Winter
               |
             Water
               |
             Phlegm
               ▽
```

Figure 3. The Relationship of Seasons, Elements and Fluids

food begins to be changed and modified as soon as it comes in contact with the lining of the mouth. Saliva also promotes digestion, due to its innate activity. Within the stomach, digestion changes food into chyme, a juice-like fluid. Chyme is absorbed through the stomach and the small intestine into the liver. Liver works rapidly with this chyme maturing it and containing within it the four primary fluids. The main characteristics of the four primary fluids are:

Sawdah – as the Arabic word indicates is black bile; it is the sediment of normal blood. Black bile corresponds to the element Earth, being cold and dry in nature and possessing a retentive force. Its taste is midway between sweetness and astringency. Black bile is associated with middle age and autumn and is active between 3 to 9 p.m. daily. The associative organs are the spleen, stomach and the blood. That bile which enters the blood is necessary for the nutrition of organs

47

such as the bones. Within the blood itself, black bile makes it thick. That bile which enters the spleen is used by the spleen for nutrition and to purify the rest of the body of its excrementitious material and part of it is sent to the stomach. It renders the stomach firm, active, and induces hunger by its acidity. Abnormal black bile can be caused by excess heat or cold, inefficiency of the spleen, dietary indiscretions such as food containing thick, dry ingredients and negative emotional conditions. There are several varieties of abnormal black bile which are a source of ill health, particularly mental-emotional diseases.

Normal **bulghum** – phlegm is sweet, associated with the element water, it is cold and moist in nature, is dominant in old age, winter and during the night from 9 p.m. to 3 a.m. The related organs are the kidneys, the bladder and the brain. It moves freely in the blood and joints. It possesses an expulsive force. Phlegm is different from the other fluids in that it can be converted into blood when necessary. It moistens the organs and joints to prevent dryness due to excess friction and heat. There are several varieties of abnormal phlegm and their main causal factors are lack of heat, working in water for long periods and an excess of phlegm-producing foods such as milk and cheese.

Normal **dam** – blood is connected to the element air, being hot and moist in nature. The associated organs are the lungs, blood and liver. Blood is active in childhood, spring and 3 a.m. to 9 a.m. Normal blood is red, sweet and without smell. Blood possesses an attractive force. Its function is to provide nutrition to the organs and tissues. Abnormal blood can result due to excess of cold and heat, due to mixture with the other fluids, dietary mismanagement or emotional imbalance.

Normal **Ṣafrah** – yellow bile, corresponding to

the element Fire, being hot and dry in nature. It is active in youth, summer and 9 a.m. to 3 p.m. during the day. Bile is light in weight, yellow in colour and possesses a digestive force. From the liver yellow bile is taken into the gall-bladder and the blood. The heart and the gall-bladder are the associative organs. That yellow bile which is taken into the blood makes the blood light and thin for easy passage through the capillaries. Yellow bile which enters the gall-bladder serves that organ and activates the intestines and rectum for defecation by peristaltic movements. Abnormal yellow bile can be due to its mixture with other fluids or due to a change of temperament. The causative factors can be excess heat, hot or sweet and greasy foods.

From these basic characteristic of the primary fluids we can begin to understand the relationship between the various factors. This simple and clear relationship begins to form a coherent picture indicating how closely and intimately interwoven are the relationship between diet, seasons, health and well-being.

MIZAJ – THE TEMPERAMENT

Mizāj – the temperament – is the dynamic state which results from the mutual interaction of the primary qualities inherent within the fluids. Every being has qualities inherent within the fluids and is endowed with the most appropriate temperament for the purpose and conditions of its creation. Human beings possess the most suitable temperament for the conditions of life. Temperament is the inherent tendency or predisposition to respond along qualitative predetermined individual characteristic patterns. Temperamental differences are the differences of response patterns to identical situations or stimuli.

Each individual reacts according to an innate psycho-emotional pattern which makes that individual unique. The concept of temperament is a central clinical consideration, significant in diagnosis and therapy. The essential sources of determining the temperament of an individual are morphological, physiochemical and psychological signs: the practical ability to determine this must be developed over many years in a clinical setting. Since the primary qualities of the elements are four, the temperament of a newly organised body is a product of the qualities of heat, cold, dryness or moisture.

Theoretically, temperament is of two kinds: balanced, when the opposing qualities are quantitatively exactly equal and the balance is an average of these qualities and imbalanced when there is a dominance of any two of the four qualities. Imbalances of temperament can be further divided into eight varieties. In a simple imbalance of temperament the dominance may be an excess of heat or cold, without any excess of dryness or moisture, or an excess of dryness or moisture, without any excess of heat or cold. However simple imbalance do not last for long as they soon become compound. An imbalance in the direction of excessive heat will promptly lead to dryness and a change in the direction of cold will increase moisture.

Compound temperaments have dominances of two qualities such as hot and moist, hot and dry, cold and moist, and cold and dry. There is no coupling of heat with cold or dryness with moisture. The above mentioned eight imbalances, four simple and four compound, have further gradations of each type into a further four degrees, depending on the strength of the imbalance. Thus in practice there can be multi-level gradation depending on the condition of the imbalance. The above imbalances can be of two kinds:

4. Physiological concepts

With morbid matter – temperament has become imbalanced due to an introduction of matter in the body such as excess phlegm or bile, etc.

Without morbid matter – these can arise per se and not from any morbid matter, e.g. cold when exposed to snow.

There are other variations such as females being generally colder in temperament than men. They have a smaller build and have more relaxed tissues and muscles. Traditionally, the human life-span on earth is divided into four broad periods:

- growth, which extends twenty-eight years,
- maturity, which lasts up to forty years,
- middle-age, which extends up to sixty years, and finally
- senility.

The period of growth is balanced in regard to heat but has an excess of moisture. During maturity there is a moderate excess of heat whilst in middle-age and old age there is an increasing proportion of cold.

THE TEMPERAMENT OF THE ORGANS

As mentioned earlier, each being as a whole is endowed with the most suitable temperament and likewise its individual parts and organs. In the case of man, each organ and member has also received the appropriate temperament requisite for its function, nature and conditions. There are some which are hot, others cold, others dry or moist. The degrees of dryness are as follows: hair is the driest of the tissues as it is formed of smoky vapours solidified by the evaporations of moisture, the darker the hair, the dryer it is. Next are the bones, which are the hardest organs. They are slightly moister than hair as they are formed of blood with much black bile and absorb moisture from the muscles attached to them. This is the reason that a number of animals derive nutrition from them, whereas this is not the case with hair. Following in a descending order of dryness are cartilage, ligaments, tendons, membranes, arteries, veins, motor-nerves, the heart, sensory nerves and skin. The coldest component of the body is the phlegm, followed by hair, bones, cartilage, ligaments, tendons, membranes, nerves, the spinal cord, breasts, testicles, lungs, liver, spleen, kidneys, muscles and skin. The hottest organ in the body is the vital force and the heart, followed by blood, liver, muscles, spleen, kidneys, the walls of the arteries and skin. As a general principle, the organs rich in blood are hot and those poor in blood are cold in temperament. As would be obvious from the gradation of various organs, skin is the most balanced constituent, and in particular the skin of the terminal phalanges.

The temperament of medicines

> *Lo! The righteous shall drink of a cup whereof the mizāj (temperament) is of camphor.*
>
> (Sūrat al-Insān, *āyat* – 5)

In traditional Islamic medicine all living objects are categorised according to temperament based on the primary qualities of heat, cold, dryness or moisture. The temperament of articles of diet, items of aesthetic value, e.g. gemstones, and medicine are generally tested on health human beings, and these tests have rigorous standards upon which Materia Medica is built. There is a system of gradation based on the degree of change that a given substance can induce within a balanced individual. There is in fact an infinite number of gradations manifested in the equally infinite number of differences between substances, as was the case with temperament within individual persons. Thus, each substance has its unique temperament, modified by climate, habitat, etc. Compound medicines also have their own temperament which, in practice becomes much more difficult to assess. Thus, in actual therapy the physician needs to be conversant with with the temperament of the articles of diet and medicine. In practice it takes many years to acquire and develop the practical art of analysis and diagnosis. We can begin to see the central importance in the evaluation of temperament in diagnosis and therapy. Specific details of signs of temperament will be discussed in a later chapter on diagnosis.

A‘ḍā’ – THE ORGANS

The structure and functions of the human body form an extensive field of study requiring years of dedicated work. In this sub-section we wish to indicate an Islamic approach to the study of anatomy and physiology, rather than to supply extensive details. The unitary nature of knowledge in the Islamic sciences can be appreciated when studying human anatomy and physiology. According to the Islamic science of medicine, every cell, tissue and organ is created in a most perfect structure to fulfil its functions. The organs are primarily formed from the co-mingling of the fluids just as the fluids are derived from the primary elements. Every organ is endowed with an innate force for nutrition by which it absorbs, retains, assimilates and integrates its own nutrition and excretes the toxic and waste matter harmful to life and health. The constituents of the human body can be divided into simple and compound organs.

The *a‘ḍā’ mufridah* are those parts in which the

visible and perceptible constituents convey the same name and definition as the whole. They are the bones, cartilage, nerves, tendons, ligaments, arteries and joints, membranes and flesh. These constituents are said to be homogeneous, as their particles or cells are of similar types[41].

A'ḍā' murakkabah are the organs of which the comprising parts, irrespective of size, differ in nature as well as name from the whole organ, e.g. hand. Thus, a part of the hand cannot be called a hand.

Compound organs are divided into a hierarchy of importance. The vital or principal organs are the heart, the brain, the liver and the generative organs. These are the centres of various functions and activities, absolutely necessary for the life of an individual and the species. The rest of the organs are auxiliary to the vital organs or are those which are instruments of their functions. The lungs are an example of the latter type. The following table indicates the two groups of auxiliary organs.

AUXILIARY ORGANS	PREPARATIVE ORGANS	VITAL ORGANS
Arteries Nerves Veins Penis, Ducts, Uterus, etc.	Lungs Stomach and Liver Stomach Generative Organs	Heart Brain Liver Testis/Ovaries

We can begin to appreciate the unitary nature of anatomy and physiology with its gradation. Information and an understanding formulated in such a manner and methodology can be helpful to a physician

[41] This is the classical way of studying anatomy and physiology.

in immediately evaluating the seriousness of any conditions upon taking up the case. Data organised in this systematic manner, based on natural laws can be of much more value in the analysis of a given individual's health-status than information derived from artificial classifications which ignore the order of creation. In this chapter a brief outline of the main physiological concepts used in traditional Islamic medicine has been described. The nature of the traditional health care approach in Islam is holistic and subtle, leading to a logical unity between the structure and function.

> All the four elements
>   are seething in this world,
> None is at rest,
>   neither earth nor fire
>   nor water nor air.
> Now earth takes the form of grass,
>   on account of desire,
> Now water becomes air
>   for the sake of this affinity.
> By way of unity,
>   water becomes fire,
> Fire also becomes air
>   in this expanse
>   because of love.
> The elements wander
>   from place to place
>   like pawns,
> For the sake of kings love,
>   not, like you,
>   for past time.
>
> *Shamsi Tabriz*

5. Life Balance

"He erected heaven and established the balance, so that you would not transgress the balance. Give just weight – do not skimp in the balance."
(Sūrat ar-Raḥmān, *āyats* – 5 -7)

Health, is a dynamic condition of balance that is the result of an individual's ability to cope with internal and external influences. The individual needs not only to create an internal balance within himself but to adapt to social, ecological and spiritual conditions[42].

The *ḥakīms* over many centuries have delineated essential factors that are fundamental to the maintenance of life and health. they are referred to as the 'six essential factors' and any imbalance in them ultimately results in disease and premature death.[43]

They are:

- Ecological conditions
- Mental and emotional aspects
- Sleep and wakefulness
- Diet and nutrition
- Physiological movement and rest
- Retention and evacuation.

---

42   One can see the holistic nature of Islamic medicine, in that it takes account of the multifarious factors acting and reacting upon an individual.

43   M.H. Shah, *The General Principles of Avicenna's Canon of Medicine*, Naveed Clinic, Karachi, 1966, p. 156.

Ecological considerations

The multiplicity of influences of the universe upon any individual are numerous, from the most, from the most subtle, such as the spirit, to the most gross, such as the sun. Air is necessary for the maintenance of life and health and is an elementary constituent of human beings. Man remains healthy as long as the air is balanced and free from pollution. Balanced air is free from fumes, chemicals, smoke and excess water vapour. Good quality air is that which is pure, clean, free from the vapours of ditches, ponds, waterlogged fields and foul gases from animal or vegetable remains. Good quality air is open to fresh breezes and comes from plains and high mountains. There are two essential functions of air:

1. conditioning
2. purification of vital force

Conditioning refers to the moderation of the temperament of the vital force. The vital force is moderated by air inhaled by air inhaled through the lungs and taken through the pores adjoining the arteries. The air that surrounds our bodies is generally much cooler than the normal temperature of the vital force. The contact and admixture of the vital force with balanced air prevents the vital force from becoming abnormal. Purification is the process whereby toxic vapours and substances are eliminated during expiration. The vital force is moderated by getting cooled during inspiration and purified during expiration.

Air has different effects depending upon its qualitative nature. Hot air is relaxing and produces dispersion. Moderate heat makes the complexion red, by drawing blood towards the surface. Excessively

5. Life Balance

hot air can turn the complexion yellow and disperses blood, producing excessive sweating and reducing the quantity of urine. It impairs the digestion and causes excessive thirst. Cold air makes the body firm, strengthens the digestion and increases the quantity of urine. Cold air hinders evacuation and prolongs stagnation. It separates water and diverts it towards the kidneys, leading to stools which are solid. Dry air makes the body thin and the skin dry and rough. Moist air softens the complexion and increases moisture.

Air can be the subject of changes which have implications for health. The changes can be normal or abnormal. Normal changes are the seasonal variations. Spring is considered the best season, as its temperament is suitable for growth and preservation of life in general and the blood and life force in particular. It is the time when the trees sprout. Spring is out of all the seasons the most balanced and has the tendency to promote natural moisture and subtle heat. It promotes a rosy complexion and activates the humours but does not disperse them as in summer. Spring is a particularly suitable season for children and puberty. During spring the activation of the humours leads to certain diseases, particularly chronic diseases. Diseases of spring are nose bleeding, rupture of blood vessels, skin conditions such as abscesses and melancholia. Individuals with a phlegmatic temperament may suffer from such diseases as apoplexy and paralysis.

Summer tends to disperse the humours and the vital force, causing enfeeblement of the bodily functions. During summer there is a decrease in the quantity of blood and phlegm with consequent changes to the quality of the humours. Bile is increased during this season, giving a yellow tint to the complexion. During the latter part of summer there is a greater accumulation of black bile due to dispersion of light humours. Diseases of summer tend to be of a short duration as the heat tends to mature and eliminate diseased matter. However in individuals of low vitality, excess heat causes debility and can lead to death. Diseases of summer tend to be due to the migration of the humours from the upper parts to the lower, such as diarrhoea. Febrile conditions are also common, as well as gangrene and infections of the eyes and ears.

Of all the seasons autumn is the one when disease is most prevalent. The reason for this is that during autumn there is less blood as it is dissipated by the other humours, leaving excessive black bile. As this periods starts to become cold there is a reduction of elimination and purification thus diverting humours inwards. Diseases in autumn are due to excess of black bile such as melancholia, cancer and joint pains. The expulsive faculty is weakened during autumn.

Winter aids digestion and is less prone to dispersion, but individuals who tend to have a sedentary lifestyle, with excessive food intake during winter are predisposed to depressive conditions. It is a period which is cold and useful for reducing bile. Winter diseases are usually phlegmatic and the common cold and its effects are prevalent at this time of the year. Winters which are particularly long and harsh are unfavourable to the old. There are also increased attacks of nervous disorders during this season.

Appropriate measures relevant to each season will be discussed in the chapter on treatment.

Mental and emotional factors

The core of an individual is the spirit which manifests itself through the mental and emotional channels. The different shades of emotions can be either positive, creative and life-enhancing or negative, destructive

5. Life Balance

and death-promoting. Each emotion, depending on its quality and severity can influence the person, in particular the vital force. In general the movement of the vital force is outward and gradual in beneficial states, such as happiness or pleasure, whereas in conditions of sorrow, depression or fear the movement of the vital force is inward. Coma or at times death can occur due to sudden inward movement of the vital force, as in shock. Any prolonged movement towards negative aspects can predispose an individual towards serious mental-emotional and physical illness.

SLEEP AND WAKEFULNESS

Sleep is an important factor in the preservation and promotion of health. The quantity and quality of sleep is a significant cause of disease. Sleep removes fatigue and regulates the flow of excretions due to the activities of the day. During sleep the innate heat is directed inwards, helping to promote digestion, growth and healing. It is due to the inward movement of the innate heat that the exterior of the sleeper becomes cold. The most beneficial sleep is that which is during the night, undisturbed, after a light, nutritious meal. Excess of sleep can dispose one to nervous diseases, dull the intellectual functions and cause accumulation of excess cold humours. Shortage of sleep is predisposed to create excess dryness with diseases such as mental confusion, itching and irritability. The effects of wakefulness are opposite to that of sleep.

DIET AND NUTRITION

Amongst the various causes responsible for ill-health are articles of food and drink individually, as well as in their different combination, have a specific effect on human health. The manner of eating, the psychological state of the person, the time of the day and year as well as the quantity and quality of food and drinks all need to be considered. In the Qur'ān foods and drinks are divided into two broad categories of *ḥalāl* – lawful and *ḥarām* – unlawful. The first category is further divided into a range of foods and drinks which are particularly health promoting and are referred to as the *ṭayyib* – wholesome. Each item of nutrition is further studied as to its qualitative aspect of being hot, cold, dry or moist. These four primary effects are then related to one of the four primary humours which may be blood, phlegm, yellow bile or black bile. The quality and quantity of food and drinks is an essential tool in the maintenance and restoration of health. If we take water as an example, as an element it is taken as part of food and drinks, enabling food towards liquefaction, transportation and absorption. There are several types of water and that which is conducive to health should have the following qualities:

- it should be light in weight;
- have a pleasant taste;
- be easily turned hot or cold;
- enable quick and easy cooking;
- have no odour or colour;
- and it should quench the thirst.

An example of water with these qualities is the water from the Zamzam spring in the valley of the Ḥijāz in Makkah.[44] The best type of water is obtained from springs where the ground is pure and free from abnormal conditions, preferably from rocky mountains which are exposed to sun and fresh air.

---

44 The water of Zamzam occupies a special curative and preventative place in Islamic medicine. One of the characteristics of Zamzam is that it is not subject to putrefaction like other waters.

Rain water collected after a storm in an area where there are no external pollutants such as gases and chemicals are also health promoting. However rain water due to its lightness, has a tendency to set up putrefactive changes. Water from snow or hail is generally impure. In hot climates or summer, ice and iced water may be used in moderation providing it is made from a pure supply of water. However individuals suffering from such conditions such as neuralgia or gastro-intestinal inflammation should refrain from iced drinks. Well water may be used, although it should be frequently lifted up from the well. Water from marshes should be avoided, as well as water containing heavy metals such as lead. Water infested with leeches and frogs is undesirable too. Specific waters rich in trace elements such as zinc or sulphur can be helpful in specific disease conditions, but must be used with caution.

Physiological movement and rest

Any form of activity whether prolonged or short, mild or vigorous, produces heat in different degrees. However, prolonged mild activity produces the greater dispersion of humours. Different occupations produce their impact on health and cause specific diseases. An occupation such as that of a washerwoman, undertaken over a long period results in a cold and moist condition whereas a blacksmith can be disposed towards excess heat and dryness. Rest is cooling and moistening, as there is little or no excitation of heat or inward accumulation of matter which subdues the heat.

Retention and evacuation

Any imbalance in retention and evacuation can be a cause towards disease. For maintenance of health there needs to be a balance between proper retention and elimination.[45] Imbalance in retention can occur when the expulsive force is weak or the retentive force is excessively strong. Improper digestion can lead to prolongation of obstruction of eliminative channels or thick viscid matter. A crisis in illness can also cause retention. Diseases of excessive retention are also moist and complex. Evacuation or loss of matter occurs when the conditions are contrary to those of retention. the diseases that occur due to excess evacuation are cold and debilitating.

---

45 The preventative measures can be rightly referred to as ecological adaptations. The modern speciality of clinical ecology is a rediscovery of the wider principles illustrated in this chapter. See R. Mackarness. *Chemical Victims*, Pan, London, 1980, pp. 1-20.

6. Diagnosis

"The Physician should be of tender disposition, of wise and gentle nature, and more especially an acute observer, capable of benefiting everyone by accurate diagnoses; that is to say, by rapid deduction of the unknown from the known; and no physician can be of tender disposition if he fails to recognise the nobility of the human being; nor of philosophical nature unless he knows logic, nor an acute observer unless he be strengthened by God's guidance."

From *Chahar Maqala* of Samarqandī

Indications of health

Before considering disease and its symptoms it is important to have an understanding of health. The signs of a healthy person with a balanced temperament are as follows:

- The complexion of an individual is pleasing with shades and colour that are normal to their respective biological environment;
- Body build is medium, neither too lean nor too heavy;
- Hair is not too profuse nor scanty;
- Feel of the body is balanced in respect of heat, cold, moisture and dryness;
- Sleep and wakefulness is moderate;

- Movements are free and easy;
- Intellectual functions and memory are good;
- Habits and behaviour are balanced between timidity and assertiveness, anger and calm, leniency and humour, pride and humility;
- Growth and repair is rapid whereas deterioration is slow;
- and dreams are interesting and pleasing.

The healthy person enjoys food, digests and assimilates normally and the excretory functions are regular.[46]

CLASSIFICATION OF DISEASES

It has been emphasised that *tibb* has an integrated approach towards health and disease in the context of spiritual, ecological and social environment. Over the centuries the practitioners of *tibb* have evolved several classifications of disease. A disease is an imbalance that disturbs the harmony and balance which is natural to human beings. A disease may be described as medical, surgical, chronic or acute depending upon its nature or treatment. However, in any disease condition the unity of the person must not be forgotten, even though that at any given moment the disturbance may be centred on a specific level or organ. There is a hierarchical division of diseases from above downward and from within outward, the most important being above and within. This gradation can be depicted in diagrammatic form, the most central and crucial being the spiritual level and the least important being the peripheral.

The most important and highest level of an individual is the spiritual level. Disturbances on this level constitute

---

46 These are the indications of health and balance, see O. C. Gruner, *The Canon of Medicine of Avicenna*, Augustus M. Kelley, New York, 1970, pp. 381-456.

6. Diagnosis

Figure 4. Hierarchical Classification of Diseases
(Spiritual, Functional, Structural, Superficial)

the most fundamental imbalance. Imbalances on this level manifest in the disturbance of the consciousness and mental functions. Conditions such as suicide, schizophrenia, delirium and total insanity are the result of disturbances on this plane.

Functional diseases are the disturbances that are manifested in imbalances of the temperament. These imbalances may be simple dominance of the active qualities of heat or cold or the passive qualities of dryness or moisture. However, simple imbalances are soon changed into compound imbalances and in this case a dominance of two qualities such as hot and moist, hot and dry, cold and moist or cold and dry comes into being. These imbalances of simple or compound type can arise either with morbid matter or without morbid matter.

Structural diseases are diseases of the structure which may be of simple organs such as the bone or compound organs like the stomach. Structural disease may affect the size, number or form of an organ.

Superficial disease are the diseases that manifest themselves on skin, hair, or other area of the complexion. Within the hierarchy this is the outermost aspect of an individual. However, the superficial diseases are the reflection of the inner working of the individual.

SIGNS OF TEMPERAMENTS

The concept of temperament is of great importance in clinical practice, particularly in diagnosis. The notion of temperament is broad enough to encompass the structural and functional aspects of an individual.[47] The signs and indications of diagnosing the temperament are many. Here we will consider the major ones.

Body build is a helpful indicator of evaluating temperament of a person. A muscular body that is well developed is a sign of heat and moisture, particularly when it is a sign of heat and moisture, particularly when it is firm and solid. Poor muscular development with deficiency of fat is an indication of dryness. Fat, flabby and cold body is a reflection of cold temperament.

Complexion is also a sign which helps in the understanding of temperament. A pale or bluish tinge is cold and shows lack of blood. Yellow complexion points to excess of heat and bile. Dark complexion illustrates heat and dryness, whereas red or rosy colour shows heat and moisture.

As well as these general signs of temperaments there are more specific indications that help in diagnosing an individuals temperament:

Hot temperament: People of hot temperament have broad chest, well-developed body with good muscular

---

47 The central clinical concept in Islamic Medicine is that of *mizāj* – temperament, evaluation of energy patterns.

growth, especially around the joints. This is due to the fact that heat promotes growth. These people are likely to have dark hair which is thick, profuse and grows rapidly. Their complexion may be dark or rosy. Their body is likely to feel hot when compared to that of a balanced person. The discharges or excretions of a person with a hot temperament are likely to have strong odours, high colour and full maturity. In individuals whose temperament is abnormally hot there may be additional signs and symptoms. They may feel uncomfortable in heat, excessive thirst, irritation and burning in the pit of the stomach, bitter taste in the mouth, intolerance of hot foods and drinks, craving of cold of cold foods and drinks and excessive anger. All of these symptoms would get worse in summer and around midday.

Cold temperament: persons of cold temperaments have the opposite signs and symptoms than those of hot-tempered individuals. Cold hinders growth and maturity and these individuals are likely to have fat bodies that feel soft, flabby and cold to touch. They are also likely to have thin, scanty hair which is slow to grow. Their complexion is more inclined towards pale or white and chalky. The excretions or discharges such as urine and perspiration are inconsistent, sluggish and without strong odour. They are more likely to be sluggish and sleep excessively. In individuals whose temperament is abnormally cold there will be additional signs of weak digestion, absence of thirst, dislike of cold drinks and foods, craving of hot drinks and foods, colds and catarrhal discharges, laxity of joints, and their symptoms becoming worse during winter and at night.

Moist temperament: People with moist temperaments are more likely to have similar symptoms to those of cold temperaments. However, in abnormally moist individuals there will be additional signs of excessive salivation, nasal discharges, diarrhoea, excessive sleep, puffiness of the body, especially under the lower eyelids, and intolerance of moist foods and habitat.

Dry temperament: Persons of dry temperaments have dryness and roughness of the skin with thin body, with prominence of joints and rapid growth of hair. In cases of abnormal dryness there may be additional indications such as insomnia, wasting, intolerance of dry foods, craving for moist foods and drinks, rapid absorption of light oils and worsening of symptoms in autumn.

Pulse

In the repository of wisdom and skills of Islamic medicine one of the subtle and important tools for evaluation of health and disease is the pulse[48]. The pulse is the movement and contraction of the heart. The purpose of this movement is to condition the vital force. Each pulse-beat consists of two movements and two pauses. Thus there is expansion followed by pause with contraction accompanied by pause. Traditionally the pulse is felt by palpating the radial artery at the wrist. The reason for feeling the pulse at this point is that it is more accessible and can be examined without embarrassment to the patient, and it is in direct continuity with the heart. It is important that when the patient is examined, the stomach should not be full and the patient should be at ease. The person examining the pulse needs to be calm and in a balanced state of health. The necessary sensitivity and practical skill in examining the person has to be developed under supervision.

---

48 I am grateful to Ḥakīm Nūr Muḥammad Hani for his help in the study of pulse diagnosis.

6. Diagnosis

The study of the pulse is complex and can be approached from different perspectives. However, here it is only possible to discuss the general principles governing the study of the pulse. The physicians have laid down a number of features that provide valuable information helpful in the evaluation of health and the diagnosis of disease:

Size: the size of the pulse is noted by examining the degree of its expansion regarding the height, length and breadth. Thus in terms of size, the pulse has nine varieties which may be medium – long or short, medium – broad or narrow and medium – low or high. A pulse is considered long if it is longer than the pulse of the hypothetical absolute balance or the normal pulse of the person himself. A long pulse is an indication of excess heat and excess of activity. A short pulse is the opposite of the long one, indicating low heat and low activity. A medium pulse is a reflection of a balanced individual. The width of pulse gives an estimate of the amount of moisture. A wide pulse indicates excess moisture, whereas a narrow pulse is the opposite, with medium being the balanced state. The depth of pulse is used to elicit the level of activity. A raised pulse points to a high level of activity with its opposite pointing to the contrary state, with the balanced level being the medium.

Temperature: the temperature of the pulse indicates the quality of the humours. A hot pulse indicates a hot quality humour, whereas a cold pulse points to a lack of heat. The moderate pulse is one showing balance.

Duration of pulse: pulse is rapid or hurried when the period between two beats is less than normal and is indicative of a fading vital force. The pulse is slow when this period is long, showing strong vital force. A medium pulse is between these two extremes.

Constancy: A pulse may continue to be constant

or vary in respect of the features illustrated above. A constant pulse is an indication of good health, whereas an irregular pulse points to weakness or disturbance. Irregular pulse can have numerous permutations too detailed to be mentioned in this work.

Strength or quality of impact: strength of the pulse gives indication of the quality of the vital force. The pulse which is felt by the pores of the fingers can be strong, which during expansion strikes forcibly against the practitioner's fingers. This variety of strong pulse indicates strong vital force. Weak of feeble pulse, the opposite of the strong type, is a pointer towards low vitality. A medium pulse is midway between the two types.

Speed or duration of cycle: speed of the pulse is an indication of a person's need for oxygen. The speed of the cycle of the pulse may be quick in which the duration of individual beats are shorter. This pulse is an indication of an individual's need for a greater amount of air. A medium type is between the two types, reflecting a balanced condition.

Consistency or elasticity: the elasticity of the pulse may be hard, pointing to excess dryness, or soft and easily compressible, reflecting excess moisture. A pulse of medium consistency is indicative of balanced moisture.

Urine

The excretion and discharges from specific organs and general body provide diagnostic indications. Urine as an example provides information about the functional states of the kidneys, digestive system, liver and spleen. However it is important to consider the following conditions:

- urine should be collected in the morning

- before any drinks or foods have been eaten;
- no substance which can alter the colour of urine should be taken, such as saffron;
- the individual giving the sample of urine should not be unduly tired or mentally excited.[49]

Important points to be considered in using urine in diagnosis are colour, density, turbidity, sediment, quantity, froth and odour. Normal urine of an adult, healthy individual is of moderate density and pale yellow in colour. It is free from an unpleasant smell, although it does have a smell. The sediments are not abnormal and there should be no irritation or burning.

The yellow colour has many shades such as orange, saffron, etc., and these different shades are an indication of over-activity and heat. Red, like yellow is also indicative of blood and heat. Any shade of green points to cold temperament as does white. Dark colouring points to excess of black bile and excessive combustion of humours.

Density of urine can be thin, medium or thick, each significant. Thick urine is a sign of defective maturation or elimination. Thick but clear urine is an indication of phlegm. Thin urine is due to incomplete maturation or weakness of kidneys, an obstruction or intake of fluids. Turbidity of urine is due to an admixture of *rīh* – gaseous air – with heavy particles. If urine is at first clear but becomes turbid on standing it indicates that the body is trying to mature the morbid matter. Turbid urine which clears upon standing but leaves a deposit of coarse particles indicates successful maturation. Turbidity of urine can also be due to elimination of matter from liver, spleen or kidneys. In such cases, the

---

[49] *The Canon of Medicine of Avicenna*, O.C. Gruner, Augustus M. Kelley, New York 1970, pp. 381-456.

findings need to be correlated with other diagnostic methods of pulse and stool.

Odour from a diseased person's urine is different from that of a healthy individual. Odourless urine is a sign of a cold temperament and immature humours. Foul-smelling urine can be a sign of ulceration in the kidneys or urinary tract. Sweet smelling urine indicates dominance of blood, whereas pungent smells point to excess of bile, acid or sour smell shows increased black bile.

The different types and amounts of sediment also provide diagnostic information. Any sample will have normal sediment and abnormal sediment such as pus. The quantity and quality of sediment is in chemical and physical aspects. In spite of adequate fluid intake scanty urine is a sign of low vitality. Passage of large quantity of urine with ease is a sign of vitality and recovery.

STOOL

Occasionally conclusions may be derived from the condition of the stool of a person. Normal stools are compact, well-formed and passed without griping or irritation at regular periods. Usually almost odourless, free from froth and faintly yellow in colour.[50] In any consideration of stool analysis, the important factor are quantity, consistency, colour and sediment which may have been eliminated from the system through the stools. Quantity may be judged by taking into account the amount of food consumed. Large stools are indicative of dominance of humours, whereas scanty stools indicate a deficiency. The liquid stools point to indigestion, weakness of mesenteric vessels or possible

---

50 *The Canon of Medicine of Avicenna*, O.C. Gruner, Augustus M. Kelley, New York 1970, pp. 355.

obstruction. Stools with froth, instead of being firm and compact, point to *rīḥ* or excess of heat. Dry stools point to cold, polyuria or intake of dry foods.

Excess change in stool colour may be indicative of a disease process. Hyperfunction of bile can change the colour of the stools to excess yellow, whereas pale stool indicates a lack of maturation. White stools can point to a lack of or obstruction of bile ducts. Black stool may point to an excess of bile which may be indicative of serious illness. Pus and blood may also be a sign of serious illness. It is important to eliminate extraneous factors such as specific foods and medication which may alter the various colours or consistency of stool.

7. Preventative aspects

"Children of Adam! wear fine clothing in every mosque and eat and drink but do not be profligate. He does not love the profligate."

(Sūrat al-Aʿrāf, *āyat* – 29)

Personal Hygiene

One of the principal objects of the Islamic health care tradition is to prevent suffering and disease prior to any clinical manifestation. The entire life is guided and directed towards wholesomeness and longevity with the emphasis on prevention. Islam as an ethical and holistic way of life deals with the spiritual and physical aspects of an individual and the community. On the spiritual and ethical levels teaching and practice harmonise the inner consciousness with the outer reality of creation. The clear and sublime perspective focuses and liberates the individual from doubt, confusion and subjugation to others and positively helps to give purpose and meaning to life. This wisdom is interwoven into daily living. A description of the daily routine will give an insight into the preventative dimension.

An individual is expected to get up early in the morning at *fajr* – dawn – before sunrise. After defecation and urination the person cleans both his hands with clean water and properly washes the anus and genital areas. The hands are then washed again, followed by the brushing of the teeth and the gums. the teeth are cleansed with *miswāk* – a traditional plant used from the early Islamic period for cleansing of teeth and oral hygiene.[51] The *miswāk* cleanses the teeth as well as having antibacterial substances destroying the harmful germs in the mouth which cause infection and tooth decay. These wooden sticks are ecological and natural as well as being safe and economical. The mouth is washed three times with clean water. Next both nostrils are cleaned internally of mucus and externally of dust. The nose is washed with clean water using the left hand. Next the whole face is washed, beginning with the forehead, both eyes and ears. The cleansing of the face is followed by washing both arms from wrist to elbows with clean running water. After this moist hands are used to clean the forehead to the back of the head. The tips of the fingers are used to clean the ears. This is completed by washing both feet up to the ankles starting from left to right, including the spaces between the toes and fingers. The *wuḍū'* – physical cleansing – is started with the clear intention of focusing the attention on the inner aspect of purification. Each stage is sanctified by the recitation of specific passages from the Qur'ān, This purification is followed by *ṣalāh* – the most sublime spiritual commencement of the day. The *ṣalāh* can be offered collectively or individually.[52]

The person stands upright with his face towards the *qiblah* – the Grand Mosque in the city of Makkah. The consciousness is directed inwards. Both hands are

[51] The Latin name of the particular tree is Salvadora Persica, whose preventative and curative value has been studied analytically in Switzerland by Pharba Basle Ltd.

[52] Al-Ghazālī, *Kimya-l-Sadat*, Sheikh Ghulam Ali & Sons, Lahore, 1977, pp. 164-83.

raised gently and then the right hand is placed on the left, just below the navel. This is followed with passages of the Qur'ān. After the recitation and contemplation the hands are placed on the knees, followed by prostration on the floor. After prostration there is a period of sitting, accompanied by contemplation and recitation. This is a brief and general sketch of the external process of a profound and powerful form of integrated worship, offered at key intervals throughout the daily cycle. There are a number of stages within *ṣalāh* – sublime prayer – focussing the individual's inner self on particular aspects. The process culminates in supplication, the essence and marrow of the whole worship.[53]

Muslim physicians have developed the use of various modes of physical exercise that act as an effective prophylactic against various diseases, as well as strengthening the body. The wisdom of exercise is profound and far-sighted. It is an established fact that every organism requires food in order to survive and preserve health. However, even if the quality of the food is wholesome and easily assimilable by the body, it does leave a certain amount of waste. The eliminative organs try to eliminate the waste and toxins, but seldom succeed in clearing all of it. The waste that is left behind gradually accumulates with potential for disease. The waste and toxins can lead to vitiation and abnormal changes in the general and specific organs, temperament, putrefaction and decay – particularly in the digestive tract – swelling and accumulation and abnormal growths.

It is these and other factors which dictate that steps need to be taken to eliminate waste and toxins. Exercise is one of the most effective and safe ways of eliminating

---

[53] Al-Ghazālī, *Kimya-l-Sadat*, Sheikh Ghulam Ali & Sons, Lahore, 1977, pp. 231. The source of this is Bukhārī.

waste products. The use of medication, unless in extreme and serious cases, is to be discouraged. Apart from the elimination of waste products, exercise stimulates the innate heat of the body, making the body stronger and lighter and building up the defences against harmful influences both external and internal. Exercise prevents the accumulation of wastes by dispersing and diverting it towards the eliminative organs and channels and assisting in expulsion of toxins. Thus with sound and regular exercise waste does not accumulate for long periods. The increase of innate heat stimulates the defences, burns out the insidious toxins and strengthens the joints and muscles. The exercise accelerates the absorption of nutrition by the tissues and organs. The organs are expanded and soften and the eliminative organs such as the skin pores are dilated. There is increased intake of oxygen, which in itself purifies and strengthens the entire body.

Exercise can be of two broad kinds: exercise carried out with the clear intention and purpose of benefiting, and exercise incidental to ordinary occupational or life activities. It is the former, proper exercise, which is the subject of our discussion and which wields maximum preventative benefits. The exercise can vary according to its mode, intensity and duration. It may be short or long, mild or strenuous, slow or rapid. It may also be rapid and strenuous or mild and slow. However, moderate exercise is the most suitable.

Strenuous exercises are many, such as boxing, wrestling, running, brisk walking, jumping, archery, fencing, horse-jumping, fighting one's shadow with a spear or a sword. The general principle of these strenuous exercises is that they are strong and vigorous. Mild exercises are carriage-riding, slow camel-riding, cruising, swinging in a lying or sitting position, etc.

7. Preventative Aspects

Bathing in different waters and massage of various types are also forms of cleansing and exercise acting as preventative measures.

There is suitable exercise for every individual according to his or her specific constitution. The light or mild exercises are appropriate for persons debilitated from diseases such as fever, and who are unable to move about quickly, or cannot stand for long periods. Persons who have used purgatives or are suffering from respiratory conditions such as pleurisy are advised to take mild exercise. The elderly are also recommended these kind of exercises and the benefits and effects of them are relaxation and sleepiness and the dispersion of *rīḥ* – harmful gases. It helps in poor memory and certain cases of brain damage, stimulates the appetite and helps in conditions of mild depression. Similarly, riding in horse-drawn carriages has beneficial effects but is slightly more potent and may produce shaking of the body. Voyaging and cruising in small vessels close to the coastline is useful in certain speech disorders and skin diseases of dry types. Cruising in deep waters can be beneficial in certain emotional conditions, but there is generation of fear.

Youth and adult life, in general, is the time for strenuous exercise as well as when specific areas need to be strengthened. There are also exercises for individual organs which have particular benefits. For the improvement of eyesight, occasional gazing at water, green plants and minute objects intently, but without fixing the eyes for too long are some examples. Listening attentively to low-pitched sounds, occasionally interspersed with high-pitched tones helps hearing. Thus each organ has a range of exercises which aid its function and structure. It is important to bear in mind that there are conditions in which exercise can be harmful and these need to be taken into consideration. The general rules are to protect the weak organs and the weak individual from strenuous exercise. In these cases exercise needs to be mild. There are some conditions such as varicose veins when movements of the part can be contra-indicated and in such conditions exercise should be given to the upper parts of the body and the legs rested. In diseases of the cerebral area, exercise of the head and neck needs to be taken with the advice of a physician. Similarly in the aged, and for pregnant women with diseases, it is advisable to consult a physician before taking systematic exercise.

There are some general rules for exercise of any type. The body needs to be in a state where food has been digested, but not empty. It should be taken at the point when the digestion is being replaced with assimilation. Before strenuous exercise there should be a warming-up period to stimulate the body gently. Massage before any exercise should be with a rough towel and after exercise with sweet oils such as almond. The bladder and bowels should be emptied before taking exercise. In hot climates or in summer it is advisable to exercise in the evening, or in summer it is advisable to exercise in the evening, or in cold climates or the winter at noon or in the morning. Exercise should be continued as long as colour is improving and the movement of limbs is easy and free, and sweat is evaporating. When these signs begin to disappear then exercise should be stopped. The end of exercise may be followed by a light massage with natural plant oils. Once a proper schedule of exercise worked out it should be continued, unless there are reasons to the contrary.

There can be a number of complications from exercise which need to be dealt with: there may be dryness,

7. Preventative Aspects

hydration, tightness, flaccidity or fatigue. Hydration can occur in individuals who live a sedentary and rich life, with frequent use of baths and much food. In these cases there should be dry massage and some recommendation of hard work. Dryness may be caused in an individual with a hot and dry temperament. In such cases rest and gentle massage with oils is the best solution. Flaccidity may be managed with a dry and vigorous massage and by use of an astringent oil. Stiffness is a frequent result of excess exercise, due to the drawing out of toxins from the tissues. Hot baths are helpful with light oil, moistening foods and rest. Fatigue is often experienced when there is excess or inappropriate exercise. Generally it disappears as soon as exercise is stopped. However, recuperative massage which directs the waste towards the skin, together with rest, helps.

Ghusl – bathing – is a necessary cleansing process which is used extensively in traditional health care. The *ḥammāms* – or baths of different kinds, are a normal feature in Muslim communities. There is extensive use of them by all sections of the community as preventative and curative aids. The particular benefits of bathing are induction of sleep, cleansing of the skin, removal of fatigue, dispersal of waste matters and drawing of blood towards the skin. Of course, indiscriminate and inappropriate use of bathing can be injurious. Excessive use may weaken the heart, produce nausea and fainting and disturb stagnant matter. General guidance with regard to bathing is to consider the season, the time of day, the condition of the stomach. Cold baths are most suitable in summer and in hot climates, whereas warm water should be used in winter and in cold regions. Cold baths should be avoided by weak, dyspeptic and cattarhal individuals.

Community health measures

Earlier in this chapter the Islamic approach to the spiritual and hygienic needs of an individual were illustrated. The balanced nature of the Islamic way life is such that it deals with the community and has a collective dimension. Indeed, the term *ummah* used to describe Muslims means 'the community'. The emphasis on communal life is an Islamic approach. The individual can only develop within a harmonious integrated and well-knit community. From the early inception of the community in Madīnah, the Prophet ﷺ regulated and paid attention to health and hygiene. The cleanliness and promotion of specific and general matters of community health constitute an important aspect of Islamic medicine. The Prophet ﷺ dealt with issues of contagion and infection. About the plague he said:

> "If you hear it has infected a certain area, stay away from it. But if it infects an area you happen to be in, do not move away from it to escape the disease."[54]

These and many other principles and practices were used in the formulation of community health policies and the organisation of environmental health. One of the central concepts and practices is the *ṭahārah* – purification.[55] The Islamic classic medical texts deal with community health under separate studies referred to as *ḥifẓ aṣ-ṣiḥḥah* – 'The Maintenance of Health'. The matters of sanitation, the quality and sources of water, the burial of the dead and other collective aspects of health are dealt with in considerable detail. Indeed there is advice to individuals attending collective

---

54 Al-Bukhārī, *Ṣaḥīḥ al-Bukhārī*, Vol. 7, Dār al-Fikr, Makkah, pp. 418-20.
55 Sūrat al-Baqarah, *āyat* – 222.

7. Preventative Aspects

prayers to refrain from eating raw onions and garlic and to use perfumes whilst attending community functions. It is the Islamic emphasis, when practised and actualised, which enabled healthy and ecologically safe communities and wider environment.

Fasting – a specific institution of health promotion

Ṣawm – complete fasting – is one institution that combined the spiritual, physical, individual and community needs in a most harmonious way. The spiritual aspect of an individual is developed and enhanced in the most potent and sublime manner. Taqwā – God consciousness, discipline and empathy with the poor and needy – are the main emphasis behind fasting. Fasting as a devotional process and internal purification enables the person to transcend his gross physical needs. The deep cleansing process clears the mind and the internal organs and tissue. Biologically, fasting is an effective, natural process of detoxification and healing. Voluntary fasting is an intensely personal process. However, the manner of fasting in the Islamic tradition is a community affair.

The period of community regulated fasting is the month of Ramadan each year. The fact that the Islamic community uses a lunar calendar gives dynamism to the whole process. The months rotate according to the various seasons over the period. The four seasons of the year change from one season to another. Thus the individual enjoys the spiritual and physical benefits both preventative and curative at different periods. The timing itself indicates the natural and dynamic adaptability of Islamic health traditions to the needs of the individual and communities over time and space.

That fasting is a potent process must be taken into

account and certain basic precautions should be noted. Children under the age of puberty are advised not to fast. Men and women who are old or have serious diseases need to consult a physician before embarking on the fast. Pregnant, or lactating women and also travellers need to be cautious and would be advised not to fast.[56]

---

[56] The *Sharīʿah* and traditions of the Prophet Muḥammad ﷺ specifically advised these categories not to fast.

8. Principles of Treatment

"Within the human being there is a morsel of flesh, and when it is corrupt the body is corrupt, and when it is sound the body is sound. Truly it is the *qalb* (the heart)."

The Prophet Muḥammad ﷺ

Management of Essential Factors

Treatment in traditional Islamic medicine consists of a number of different therapies selected and adapted to both the general and the specific needs of the individual patient. The various levels of treatment are management of essential factors, use of medicaments, psycho-spiritual healing, manipulative measures and surgical intervention. The management of essential factors which was discussed in the chapter on pathogenesis provides broad options capable of restoring balance without the use of medicaments. Management of the 'six essentials', as they are known sometimes, consists of suitable modification. Food, one of these factors, can be considered to illustrate this, using general principles for managing the quality and quantity of food as a therapeutic measure. *Ṭibbī* – medicinal – nutrition, is based on the concept that for each food, whether it is fruit, vegetable or meat, there is an energy, essence or state of quality that can be identified and formulated. The quality of the foods can be formulated by using the energy conceptual framework. This enables the physician to express the essence of food in a holistic manner and context.

In nutritional therapy, food can be withheld, increased, or given in moderate quantity, depending upon the needs and conditions of the individual patient and the nature of the disease. Food serves to provide energy and replaces the loss that results from the various activities of life and living. From an Islamic perspective there are the interconnections between food and the states of consciousness and emotional processes. In any disease there is an imbalance that also disturbs the various aspects of a person. The fact that an individual is considered as one dynamic and integrated whole helps us to see the interconnections. Food is one of the most potent and yet safe instruments of establishing balance in a disturbed organism. Each individual ingredient in food is studied and understood in the holistic conceptual and empirical framework which was discussed in earlier chapters. The *ḥakīms* classify the range of foods on their qualitative basis of hot or cold and dry or moist. The qualitative nature of foods are part and parcel of common knowledge and folk traditions within Islamic communities. Traditionally, the selection of foods is based on season, age and needs of the individual. The therapeutic use of foods consists of using the qualitative understanding and quantity in a sensitive and controlled manner. A diet consisting mainly of fruit and vegetables is different in quality from, for example half boiled eggs and meats. Individuals with hot diseases such as fevers need essentially to use cooling vegetables of leafy types. Individuals with a good appetite but immature humours should be encouraged to change to a bulky diet. This will satisfy the appetite without adding to the quantity of the humours.

8. Principles of treatment

The quantity of food is generally reduced or stopped in acute diseases and sometimes chronic conditions. In chronic conditions, the strength and vitality has been lost for considerable time and has to be maintained by the supply of food. In acute diseases however, the crisis occurs quickly and it is expected that the strength will be sufficient to turn it into a healing crisis, culminating in health. The regulation of food at the critical stage of the disease, when the vital force is actively engaged in the struggle, requires a light diet. Indeed, the more acute the illness and the nearer the time of crisis, the lighter the food should be, unless there are contra-indications.

Other factors in food management which are taken into consideration are rate of digestion and absorption of foods. Heavy and viscid foods such as beef are avoided in cases of stasis and obstruction. Assimilable and energy-giving foods such as honey are included when there is such a need in conditions following prolonged illness. The psychological states and physiological conditions of an individual are also important considerations. The symbolic relationship of foods derived from cultural and religious sources must also be taken into account when planning any food therapy with an individual patient.

TREATMENT THROUGH A SINGLE REMEDY

In Islamic medicine there is a distinction between *mufradāt* – single – and *murakkabāt* – compound medicaments.[57] The traditional use of individual substances in the treatment of various diseases still continues to be practised as therapy of choice today. The range of substances used in the alleviation of suffering reflects the wide range of the richness that

---

[57] This is a classical division of Materia Medica by Muslim physicians and scholars.

exists in Nature's treasury. Although remedies may be used from the mineral, plant and animal kingdoms, in practice, most remedies come from plant sources. In treatment, the principle that each human being is a reflection of all creation is followed by using a whole range of substances. Thus the analogy of micro-macro constitutes a biological reality and also has application in medical practice.[58] The use of the individual remedy is based on sound theoretical foundations and is supported by observation and experiments of countless generations of reputable physicians. Such empirical knowledge and wisdom, particularly in pharmacognosy is considerable and constitutes important skills in Islamic medical practice. The general emphasis in planning medicament therapy is to re-establish the lost balance within an individual patient with minimum intervention and change. The medicaments are used and selected after meticulous and comprehensive life history, with particular reference to the medical aspects of an individual patient in the context of their family. The remedies are used in an active biological state rather than isolating a specific chemically or pharmacologically active element. The physician has to know each specific remedy in full detail. The physician must know the:

- name of the remedy;
- identification and study of its natural habitat;
- nature of the remedy;
- specific energy pattern;
- physiochemical actions;
- indications of its uses in general and specific conditions;

---

[58] The research in our own age is also moving towards this realisation that human beings contain the different energies and physiochemical constituents of the earth.

8. Principles of treatment

- specific relationship to organs;
- duration of its action;
- toxicity and contra-indications;
- types of preparation;
- And dosage, administration and antidote.

The modes of administration are many, depending on factors such as the nature of the disease, organ, etc. The general principle is to use medicine in a condition that is effective but without any harmful side-effects. There are a range of preparations such as infusions, decoctions, tinctures, extracts, tablets, pills, elixirs, electuaries and oils, with ointments and creams for external applications. The whole range of different parts of plants are used including roots, rhizomes, stems, barks, leaves, flowers, gums and oils.

Selection of the remedy depends upon the understanding and evaluation of an individual patient's temperament, the nature, severity and location of the disease. The physician also has to consider the sex, age, season, lifestyle, residence, occupation and previous treatment of the individual patient. Each of the above factors has to be applied in order to restore the lost or displaced equilibrium. An unbalanced organ provides and illustrative example. If the practitioner considers that an organ is diseased, then whilst paying attention to the other factors he has to select a single medicine with regard to the temperament of the organ affected, its structure, position and vitality.

Temperament is the energy pattern of the organ and provides information of the highest importance. When the original and normal energy pattern of the affected organ is known, it is relatively easy for the practitioner to assess the extent of abnormality and appropriate dosage and potency. If the affected organ is of hot temperament and the disease is cold, it indicates gross abnormality which will require strong, hot doses. However, if the original temperament is cold and the disease is also of the same quality then mild, cooling doses will re-establish the lost balance. The position and relationship of the affected organ is important too. Anatomical knowledge is helpful in the selection of the mode of administration of a remedy. The position of an organ can give an indication of the accessibility of an organ for remedial action. For example, the stomach is more easily influenced by mild medicament than the lungs. Each organ has interrelationships with other organs which help in determining treatment. The relationship of the liver to the kidneys and stomach is a useful example. If there is morbid matter in the upper part of the liver it can easily be eliminated through the kidneys, whereas if it is in the lower part of the liver it is better disposed of through the bowels. Correspondingly, the structure of an organ will give information which will indicate the level of penetration and absorption. Spongy organs respond differently to medicine from solid ones. The vitality of an organ is a significant factor in planning any treatment. The fundamental or vital organs such as the heart, brain and liver need milder medicine as any disturbance or too rapid change can cause serious complications. The vitality of an organ can also give and indication of the level of morbid matter and toxicity. Sensitivity and the normal function of the organ also have to be considered in the selection of a single remedy so as to avoid irritation or possible injurious effects.

Use of compound medicines

The use of compound medicaments is also employed in the treatment of internal diseases of complex and

8. Principles of treatment

chronic nature. In traditional Islamic medicine, although the general preference is for the single remedy there are diseases in which using more than on substance combined in a coherent and thought-out basis enables a speedier cure. There are certain medicines which when used singly, even if in limited amounts have certain undesirable side-effects. Muslim practitioners developed this branch of the art and published authoritative works such as *Aqrabadin* – Pharmacopeia. The classical Greek and Indian sources were particularly utilised in the development of the use of compounds by Muslim physicians, and continue to be prepared and manufactured in the traditional methods by individual practitioners and natural medicine companies.[59] Works by masters of Islamic medicine such as Ibn Sīnā and ar-Rāzī's works continue to be used as basic references by today's practitioners. With the emergence of new stress deficiencies and patterns of disease there are formulations which take into account the new conditions. Generally only reputable *ḥakīms*' formulations are used. Usually the formulation or change in any traditional forms is a complicated process requiring a deep understanding of Materia Medica, and of human diseases, as well as considerable experience.

THE USE OF THE QUR'AN IN HEALING

An essential feature of the philosophy and practice of Islamic medicine is its harmony and ability to respond to the total needs of human beings. Islamic medicine has many facets which, one the one hand, relate to the physical needs and on the other hand are intimately bound with the higher order, and are

---

[59] Dawākhānah Ḥakīm Ajmal Khān Ltd. of Lahore, *Methods of Medicament Preparations*.

responsive to the intangible aspects of the person. The whole phenomenon of creation is one that has the potential of uplifting and promoting creativity as well as the ability to degrade and debase. The existence and influence of destructive forces are also acknowledged, in particular the causes of insidious diseases of psycho-spiritual origin.

The Qur'ān depicts this reality in vivid language in a number of places:

> "*Say: I seek refuge in the Lord of the Daybreak,*
>
> *From the evil of what he has created;*
>
> *From the evil of darkness when it gathers;*
>
> *From the evil of conjuring witches;*
>
> *From the evil of the envier when he envies.*"
>
> (Sūrat al-Falaq)

This awareness and understanding of the cosmological situation has enabled the *ḥakīms* to respond to diseases requiring intervention on a higher level. The Islamic Sharīʿah – Divine Law – prohibits the practice and use of *siḥr* – magic – in treatment. The Qur'ān in its totality, and certain sections and verses in particular, is curative of serious conditions and verses in particular, is curative of serious conditions not amenable to other forms of treatment.[60] Muslim physicians use guidance and specific verses from the Qur'ān in treatment. The methods of using the Qur'ān are many. They are:

- *Taʿwīdh* – literally meaning 'refuge' – in which sections of the Qur'ān are used;
- *Daʿwah* – invocation;
- and *Ruqyah* – 'charms'.

---

60   Sūrah Ṭāhā, *āyat* – 69.

8. Principles of treatment

are methods in which specific verses of the Qur'ān are used in particular sequence and recited.[61]

SURGICAL INTERVENTION

Surgery has been an integral part of the practice and study of traditional Islamic medicine. Physicians were trained both in surgery and internal medicine. It was during Abū'l-Qāsim az-Zahrāwī's time that the practice of surgery reached its zenith. His classical work on the art. *Kitāb at-Taṣrīf* – The Method of Medicine – dealt with the subject in detail. Az-Zahrāwī for the first time drew each instrument in colour. The general misunderstanding, namely that controlled dissection of the human body in the Islamic community prevents the growth and development of anatomical and physiological knowledge, is inaccurate. The study of human form has been an important aspect of Muslim scholarship to the extent that philosophers and mystics like al-Ghazālī thought it important in their gnostic traditions. Indeed, physicians and surgeons, for instance Ibn an-Nafīs, were aware of the lesser circulation in 687 A.H. (1288 C.E.).[62] Muslim surgeons used and developed a wide range of surgical instruments which were not only useful but beautiful and artistic in their looks. There were a number of surgical procedures that were used, from Caesarian section to complicated eye operations. The Muslim surgeon Thābit ibn Qurrah was using *tanwīm* – anaesthesia – in operations of the eyes as early as 850 A.H. (1492 C.E.).[63] The present situation in traditional Islamic medicine schools, unfortunately,

---

[61] A. Ali, *Amal-I-Qurani*, Naz Publishing House, Delhi p. 15.

[62] S.H. Nasr, *Science and Civilisation in Islam*, Harvard University Press, 1969 p. 213.

[63] M. Bayrakdar, 'The First Use of Anaesthesia', Imam, 1984, pp. 52-3.

does not reflect this outstanding surgical knowledge. Since colonial subjugation, in particular, the level of knowledge and skills of *ḥakīms* in surgery declined to such an extent that it may be said to be non-existent.[64]

---

[64] The reasons are many for this situation, with the most apparent being that the government is reluctant to fund surgery in traditional colleges as well as the Muslim physicians' own lack of surgical skills.

9. The Future of Islamic Medicine

"We will soon show them Our signs in the Universe and in their own souls, until it will become quite clear to them that it is the truth. Is it not sufficient as regards your Lord that He is a witness over all things?

"Now surely they are in doubt as to the meeting of their Lord; now surely He encompasses all things."

(Sūrah Fuṣṣilat, *āyats* – 53-54)

Sociocultural implications

In this final chapter, the focus will be to consider the future role of the Islamic health care tradition for health, well-being and its sociocultural, economic and peace implications and benefits. Of course, these considerations do not constitute part of the accepted body of Islamic medical knowledge.

Given the prohibitive cost of technologically-based medicine, its inability to cure increasing chronic diseases, and the rising dissatisfaction – to the point of alienation – on the part of the intelligent public, a positive and important future is indicated for Islamic medicine.[65] The holistic and liberating paradigms, long clinical and therapeutic experiences, with a gentle efficacious and rich treasury of natural medicaments,

---

[65] S. Fulder and R. Monr, *The Status of Complementary Medicine*, The Threshold Foundation, London, 1981, pp. 1-19. This and many other reports and publications indicate the need for holistic health care.

places Islamic medicine as the medicine of the future. It is surprising to what extent a tradition of health care with such positive characteristics as Islamic medicine has been hidden and ignored, and it would perhaps be helpful to consider why this has happened to such an economical and natural medicine.

The breakdown of Islamic culture was followed by subjugation and colonial domination. The colonial powers successfully disintegrated and fragmented most of the remaining Muslim societies. This physical disintegration was followed by the destruction of economic, political and sociocultural and scientific structures. The traditional colleges of Islamic medicine, hospitals and professional organisations were systematically deprived of essential resources and freedom to practice and develop. The status and positive images of the ḥakīms and ṭabībs – physicians, were degraded. In a number of countries in the Muslim world their practices and teachings were made unlawful.[66]

However, the grassroots popularity of Islamic medicine and its appeal and practical usefulness, enabled it to be practised in various forms. The practice and teaching was well organised and deep-rooted in India, Bangladesh, Malaysia and Pakistan.[67] The political independence of Muslim lands has been accompanied by increasing awareness of cultural and scientific traditions and heritage. The Islamic reconstruction has also begun to give prominence to Islamic sciences, including medicine.[68] The need for

66 In parts of the Arabian peninsula even today ḥakīms are not allowed to practice or set up professional organisations.
67 India and Pakistan are the leading pioneers in promoting Islamic Medicine with central and regional government funding.
68 The Islamic Medicine Organisation (I.M.O) in Kuwait is an example as well as the work of Ḥakīm Muḥammad Sa'īd, President of the Hamdard Foundation, Karachi, Pakistan. See also Z. Sardar, *Science*

9. The future of Islamic medicine

appropriate and effective medical care for masses of people provides new impetus for the future of Islamic medicine.

ECONOMIC CONSIDERATIONS

Today, the practice of medicine is a major economic enterprise. The medical industry of our time is one of the largest and most powerful multinationals, particularly the pharmaceutical companies. The mechanistic approach of the dominant medical schools has led to a huge and cumbersome technological industry for diagnosis and treatment which knows no limits. Within the industrialised nations of Europe and the United States of America there is increasing dissatisfaction with the high technology medical matters which alienates the patients from their practitioners. The human dimension of care and sensitivity has been replaced by intrusive and insidious machines. The medical technology and pharmaceutical drugs sap away major chunks of the health care budget. The toxic side effects of drugs and most forms of mechanical diagnosis are becoming a health menace. Government and research scholars are beginning to alert the public to the economically unsuitable health service and there is now serious re-assessment of the whole basis of health care.[69] Indeed there is tremendous interest in, and growth of, human oriented and economical health alternatives within most industrialised nations. Given these considerations it is important that non-industrialised nations maintain and develop traditional health care resources.

---

and Technology in the Middle East, Longman, London, 1982, pp. 18-23.

69 I. Kennedy, *The Unmasking of Medicine,* George Allen & Unwin, London, 1981, pp. 117-69.

Implications for peace and happiness

The present age can be appropriately said to be the age of tranquillisers and violence. Each day some new tranquilliser is invented and introduced into the already extensive toxic armoury of chemical drugs, promising the ever-elusive state of peace and tranquillity. However, the range and level of mental and emotional disturbances and diseases are on the increase. The manifold stress of industrial life, a toxic environment and subversive, drug based medicines compound the agony and suffering towards insanity and complete disintegration of the core of human beings. Highly mechanised hospitals with numerous specialists themselves appear to be victims of the process of dehumanisation by modern technocratic medicine. It is in this desperate context that Islamic medicine can provide the primordial wisdom, healing and creative energy with its gentle and effective treasury of natural medicine. The agonised and suffering masses could benefit enormously through the holistic and natural tradition of Islamic medicine. It is the benevolent Creator who has created relief for mankind through His mercy and love. True health, peace and happiness comes through unification with the Truth.

GLOSSARY

iʿtidāl: A dynamic condition of balance and equilibrium.

akhlāṭ: The four biological fluids, blood, phlegm, bile and black bile. these constitute the biological bases of Islamic medicine.

ʿaql: An apprehending light, unique to human beings which guides the individual towards balanced decisions and actions.

Aqrabadin: A pharmacopoeia of compound medicine giving details of individual substances and directions for their manufacture and use.

arkān: The four basic elements, fire, air, water and earth.

āyat: A Qur'ānic term which means signs and manifestations, which, when reflected upon, guide towards purpose and meaning.

Bayt al-Ḥikmah: The House of Wisdom, an academy founded in Baghdad by the Abbassids to promote the systematic research and development of sciences.

Bimaristan: A place for the sick, a hospital.

bulghum: Phlegm, one of the four primary biological fluids, associated with water and being cold and moist in nature.

ẓāhir:	The external or outward aspects of creation and existence.
diyah:	Blood money paid in compensation for a homicide.
dīn al-fiṭrah:	The primordial tradition and way of life, Islam.
ghayb:	The hidden or unseen aspect of existence which beyond normal human sensory perceptions.
ḥakīm:	An individual endowed with knowledge experience and wisdom, a sage. The title is given to a consultant physician of Islamic medicine.
ḥalāl:	Lawful and permitted food, nutrition and behaviour which is life giving.
ḥammām:	A bath, generally deep cleansing warm and cold alternating.
ḥarām:	Opposite of *ḥalāl*, unlawful, destructive nutrition or behaviour.
ḥifẓ aṣ-ṣiḥaḥ:	Hygiene and public health matters with emphasis on prevention of ill health.
jism:	The material body.
khamr:	Intoxicants, that which covers up the reason, alcohol.
laṭīf:	Subtle and penetrative force.
miswāk:	A traditional root, used from the time of the Prophet Muḥammad ﷺ.
mufradāt:	Individual drugs, usually of plant origin, in their natural states. Class of Islamic medical literature, which deals with the study and uses of natural substances.
murakkabāt:	Compound medicines, prepared from a number of individual substances. A class of Islamic medical texts dealing with the use and manufacture of compound medicines.

Glossary

mizāj:	A dynamic functional state which reflects the energy pattern of an individual person or thing.
nafs:	The self, which can be in a number of states: *Nafs ul Ammārah* – fossilised and insensitive; *Nafs ul-Lawwamah* – reproachful and agitated; *Nafs ul-Mutma'innah* – tranquil or balanced state.
qalb:	An immaterial principle – which regulates the predominantly psycho-emotional life of a person.
rīḥ:	A harmful type of gaseous wind, usually in the stomach.
rūḥ:	The vital force, a purposeful and dynamic force that permeates the human organism. Muslim physicians give different names to it depending on its function and location: *Ḥawānīyyah* – centred in the heart and maintains life; *Nafsīyyah* – located in the brain and promotes sensation in movement; and *Ṭabbayyah* – located in the liver for the preservation of the individual and in the ovaries and testicles for the preservation of the species.
Rūḥ:	The spirit which is of divine origin and is transcendental.
ṣafrah:	Yellow bile, one of the four primary biological fluids corresponding to the element of fire and hot and dry in nature.
sakīnah:	A state of peace and tranquillity; the result of unification with the truth.
sawdah:	Black bile, one of the four primary biological fluids corresponding to the

	element of earth and cold and dry in nature.
sharīʿah:	A path, paradigm of principles and practices which enables human beings to live in harmony with reality.
ṭahārah:	Purity and cleanliness of an individual and community.
taqwā:	A state in consciousness which guides one to refrain from destructive behaviour.
ṭibb:	Literal meaning 'nature' refers to holistic medicine.
aṭ-ṭibb an-nabawī:	Prophetic medicine.
waḥy:	Revelation, that is direct knowledge from the Creator.

INDEX

A

ʿAbbās ibn ʿAbd al-Muṭṭalib 17
ʿAbd ar-Raḥīm ad-Dakhwar 21
Abū ʿImrān Mūsā ibn Maymūn 17, 21
Abū Bakr ibn Samghūn 16
Abbasids 17, 18, 19, 20
Abū'l-Ḥasan al-Andalūsī 16
Abu'l-ʿAbbas ʿAbdullah as-Saffāḥ 17
aʿḍāʾ mufridah 54
aʿḍāʾ murakkabah 53, 54
Ahwaz 18
air 44-46, 48, 55, 58-59
Ajmal Khān, Ḥakīm 93
Akbar Arazani 22
ākhirah 35
akhlāṭ 37, 46
āyats 1, 29
ṣalāh 79
al-akhlāṭ al-arbaʿah 46
amānah 31
anaesthesia 95
Anatolia 22
Andalusia 16
ʿaql 40
Aqrabadin 93

Arabia 3
Arabian Peninsula 3
Arabian Sea 3, 5
arkān 44
Auxiliary Organs 54
Avicenna *see* Ibn Sīnā
Ayindoglu Umar Bey 22
Ayurvedic physicians 22

B

Baghdad 17, 19, 20, 21
balance 32
Basra 17
Bayt al-Ḥikmah 19
bile 51, 75
    black bile 46, 47, 52, 59, 62
    yellow bile 46, 49, 62
Bimaristān 18
blood 46, 48, 59, 62
Bukhara 20
Bukt Yishu 18
bulghum, see phlegm

C

Cairo 21
Chahar Maqala 65
Chinese 1
chyme 47

105

Complementary Medicine 97
compound medicaments 53, 89, 92
Cordoba 16, 21

D

daʿwah 94
dam 46, 48
Damascus 18, 21
Dar al-Funūn 21
Dhakhīrah Y Khwarzam 21
dīn al-fiṭrah 27
Dioscorides 16
diyah 12
Dr. Bernard 22
dreams 66
dunyā 35

E

earth 31, 44, 45, 47, 55
Egypt 21, 22
The Elemental Dance 1
elephant 25
Elgood 18
European medicine 21
exercise 79, 80, 81
ex-nihilo 28

F

fajr 77
fasting 85
Fatimids 21
Firdaws al-Ḥikmah 19
fire 44-46, 49, 55

G

Galen 19
ghāʾib 29, 39
al-Ghazālī 28, 35, 78, 79, 95

Ghengis Khān 20
ghusl 83
God consciousness 85
growth 51
Gulf of Aden 3
Gulf of Oman 5

H

Muḥammad Ajmal Khān, Ḥāfiẓ 23
Hae Pasha, Ḥakīm 22
Hahnemann 57
ḥakīms 32, 33, 57, 88, 93, 94, 96, 98
ḥalāl 62
Hamdard Foundation 98
ḥammāms 83
ḥarām 62
al-Ḥāwī 20
heart 35, 52, 87
ḥifẓ aṣ-ṣiḥḥah 84
Ḥijāz 62
Hippocrates 19, 77
Hulagu 20
human being 1, 31, 32
Ḥunayn ibn Isḥāq 19

I

ʿibādah 31
iʿtidāl 32
Ibn ʿArabī 28
Ibn Abi ʿUsaybiah 21
Ibn al-Bayṭār 16
Ibn an-Nafīs 95
Ibn Bājah 16
Ibn Rushd 16, 17
Ibn Sīnā, Abū ʿAlī 20, 32, 37, 57, 66, 73, 74, 93
Ibn Ṭufayl 16, 17
individuation faculty 38

Index

Indo-Pakistan subcontinent 22
insān 1, 32
al-Insān al-Kabīr 30
intuition 40
Iran 21, 22
Isa Canal 18
Islamic Medicine 98
Islamic Medicine Organisation 98

J

Jāmiʿ li Mufradāt al-Adwiyā' wa al-Aghdhiyā' 16
Jalāluddīn Rūmī 25
Jazīrat al-ʿArab 3
Jibrīl Bukht Yishu 19
jism 35
Jundishapur Medical School 18, 19
Jurjis Ibn Bukht Yishu 18

K

Karkh 18
Karkhaya Canal 18
khalīfah 1
Khorosan 18
Khwarzam 21
Kitāb al-ʿAshr Maqālāt fi'l ʿAyn 19
Kitāb al-Aghdiyah 16
Kitāb al-Asbāb wa'l-ʿAlāmāt 21
Kitāb al-Fuṣūl 17
Kitāb at-Taṣrīf 16, 95
Kitāb at-Taysīr fi'l-Mudāwāt wa't-Tadbīr 16
Kitāb Tadbīr aṣ-Ṣiḥḥah 17
Kufa 17

L

laṭīf 37
al-Laṭīf al-Baghdādī 21
leucoderma 38
liver 47

M

macrocosm 29, 30
Madīnat az-Zahrā' 16
Maimonides, *see* Abū ʿImrān Mūsā ibn Maymūn
Makkah 62, 78
Malaga 16
Mankha 19
al-Manṣūr, Abu Jaʿfar 17, 18
Masīḥ al-Mulk 23
Materia Medica 16, 52, 89, 93
Mathnāwī 25
maturity 51
Mediterranean 5
Method of Medicine 95
microcosm 29, 31
miswāk 78
mizāj 43, 49, 52, 68
Mogul India 22
morbid matter 51
mufradāt 89
Muḥammad Nabi Khān, Ḥakīm 23
Muḥammad Riaz Qersih Ṣāḥib, Ḥakīm 23
Muḥammad Saʿīd, Ḥakīm 98
Nūr Muḥammad Hani, Ḥakīm 70
Muḥammad Hussain, Ḥakīm 23
murakkabāt 89

N

Nadir Shah 21
nafs 30, 35-36
an-nafs al-ammārah 36
an-nafs al-lawwāmah 36
an-nafs al-mutma'innah 36
natural faculty 38
nervous faculty 39
nutrition 87

O

ophthalmologist 19
Ottoman Turkey 22

P

Persian 1, 22
Persian Gulf 3, 5
pharmacognosy 90
Pharmacopeia 93
phlegm 46, 48, 51-52, 59, 62
plague 84
Pre-Islamic Arabia 3
Preparative Organs 54
Prophet Muḥammad ﷺ 1, 86-87
purgatives 81

Q

qalb 35, 87
qiblah 78
al-Qānūn fi't-Ṭibb 20
quwwah 43
al-quwwah al-mughayarah 38
quwwah mutafakkirah 40
al-quwwah an-nāṭiqiyah 40

R

rūḥ 35, 37

rūḥ ṭabayyah 38
Rai 20
Ramadan 85
rational mind 40
rūḥ ḥaywāniyyah 38
ar-Rāzī, Muḥammad ibn Zakariyyā 18, 20
Red Sea 3
Renaissance 27
rīḥ 73, 75, 81
Rūmī 26
rūḥ nafsāniyyah 39
ar-Rubʿ al-Khālī 5
ruqyah 94

S

Saffavid 21
ṣafrah, see bile, yellow
sakīnah 31
ṣalāh 78
Salahudin 17
Saliva 47
Salvadora Persica 78
Samarqand 20, 21
as-Samarqandī, Abu Ḥāmid Muḥammad 21, 65
sawdah, see bile, black
ṣawm 85
Sayyid Hossein Nasr 35
Sayyid Zayn ad Dīn Ismāʿīl al-Ḥusaynī al-Jurjānī 21
self, *see nafs*
senility 51
Shahādah 28
Shamals 5
Shamsi Tabriz 55
Sharīʿah 86, 94
Shifā' al-Mulk 23
single medicaments 89
siḥr 94

six essential factors 57
smallpox vaccinations 22
spirit 35
Sultan Maḥmūd II 22
surgery 95
as-Suyūṭī 12
Syrian Desert 3

T

ṭabībs 98
Ṭā'if 5
ta'wīdh 94
tanwīm 95
taqwā 85
tawḥīd 28, 35
ṭayyib 62
temperament 49, 68, 69, 70, 91
Thābit ibn Qurrah 19, 95
thinking 40
ṭibb 66
aṭ-Ṭibb al-Akbar 22
aṭ-Ṭibb al-Islāmī 32
aṭ-Ṭibb an-Nabawī 1
Ṭibb an-Nabī 12
Tigris 17
Turkey 22

U

Umayyads 17
ummah 84
Urdu 22

V

vital faculty 38
vital force 37, 39, 52, 57, 58
vital organs 54

W

wahm 40
water 8, 44-45, 48, 55, 59, 62-63, 77-78, 81, 83-84
waḥy 28
wuḍū' 78

X

xerophytic 5

Y

Yuhanna ibn Masawayh 19

Z

ẓāhir 29, 39
az-Zahrāwī, Abu'l-Qāsim 16, 95
Zamzam 62